CONNECT WITH
THE HEART
OF GOD

A GUIDE FOR THE LETTER TO THE HEBREWS

CONNECT WITH THE HEART OF GOD

CHARLES PRICE

LIVING TRUTH

experiencing Christ in you

Contents

Preface

It was a great privilege to have been invited by the trustees of the annual Keswick Convention to give a series of messages on the New Testament book of Hebrews to the several thousands of people in attendance from all over Britain.

The Convention has been an annual event in the English Lake District town of Keswick since 1875, and through it countless people have met with God in a life-changing way. It's goals are greater holiness of life and more effectiveness in service, and the means to that goal is the clear and faithful exposition of Scripture in dependence on the Holy Spirit of God.

I am delighted that these five messages have been put into book form, with the tremendous help of Elizabeth McQuoid, who edited the manuscript, divided it up into manageable sections, devised the questions and suggestions for further study and made it many times more useful than it otherwise would have been. Because the material was originally spoken in a public setting over five days, the style is informal and sometimes local. There are of course sections of Hebrews which deserve much fuller treatment than time permitted, but which had to be passed over in the hope of hitting the high peaks.

May God use it to connect you more fully with the rich life available to us in Jesus Christ.

Charles Price
Toronto, Canada

THE AIM OF THIS STUDY GUIDE

The aim of this study guide is to uncover the message of the letter of Hebrews. Charles Price invites us to join those first century believers and 'fix our eyes' and 'fix our thoughts' on the Lord Jesus. The questions that follow help relate the principles he draws out to our own lives and situations. You can use this guide either for your own devotional time with God or as a part of a group. Enjoy your study!

USING THIS BOOK FOR PERSONAL STUDY

Begin by praying and reading through the passage and commentary a number of times before looking at the questions.

You may find it helpful to note down your answers to the questions and any other thoughts you may have. Putting pen to paper will help you think through the issues and how they specifically apply to your own situation. It will also be encouraging to look back over all that God has been teaching you.

Talk about what you're learning with a friend. Pray together that you'll be able to apply all these new lessons to your life.

USING THIS BOOK IN SMALL GROUPS

Aim to cover one chapter of the study guide per session. If you don't have the time to cover all fourteen chapters, just focus on those chapters that are most appropriate to the needs of your group.

In preparation for the study, pray and read the passage of Scripture and commentary over a number of times. Use other resource material such as a Bible dictionary or atlas if they would be helpful.

Each week, think through what materials you need for the study – a flip chart, pens and paper, other Bible translations, worship tapes.

At the top of each chapter we have stated the aim – this is the heart of the passage and the truth you want your group to take away with them. With this in mind, decide which questions and activities you should spend most time on. Add questions that would be helpful to your group or particular church situation.

Before people come, encourage them to read the passage and commentary that you will be studying that week.

Make sure you leave time at the end of the study for people to 'Reflect and Respond' so they are able to apply what they are learning to their own situations.

Introduction

You may have heard the story of the occasion when Sherlock Holmes and his sidekick, Doctor Watson, went camping in the Lake District. After they'd set up their tent and had a good dinner, they retired for the night. Some hours later, Holmes woke up, nudged his faithful friend and said, 'Watson, wake up.' Watson opened his eyes and Holmes said, 'Watson, what do you see?' Watson looked up and said, 'I see millions and millions of stars.' 'What do you deduce from that?' Holmes asked him. Watson pondered for a moment and said, 'Well, astronomically, it tells me there are millions of galaxies and billions of stars. Astrologically, I observe that Saturn is in Leo. Horologically, I deduce that it's about quarter past three in the morning. Meteorologically, I suspect we're going to have a beautiful day tomorrow. Theologically, it tells me God is great and all-powerful and we're just insignificant parts of his creation. Why, what does it tell you, Holmes?' Holmes was silent for a moment and then said, 'Watson, you idiot, it means somebody's stolen our tent.'

I tell that story because there are some things in life that are so obvious we miss them, we take them for granted. And in our journey through the letter to the Hebrews, I want to look at something that is so fundamental and so obvious that, in actual fact, many of us miss the significance of it. In a nutshell, it is the supremacy of Christ in divine revelation, and the sufficiency of Christ in Christian experience. The writer to the Hebrews tells us Christ is not just a contributor to divine revelation. He is the arbitrator of divine revelation; he is the ultimate and the final expression of truth. But he's also sufficient in Christian experience. He doesn't just play a passive role in our Christian lives, he's not just an onlooker or a spectator, he is the central participant.

Sometimes we relegate Christ to being little more than the patron of our theology: we do things in his name but we've become detached from him. Sometimes we relegate him to being the teacher who's left us here to work out his teaching. Sometimes we relegate him to being the example that we try to emulate and follow. And there are elements of truth in all of this. But that's also the role that Muhammed plays in Islam and he's dead. It's the role any religious leader plays in any new religion. As we explore this letter to the Hebrews we'll find that the role of Jesus Christ is so much fuller and so much more active. Hebrews 3:1 says, 'Therefore, holy brothers, who share in the heavenly calling, fix your thoughts on Jesus, the apostle and high priest whom we confess.' And 12:2 'Let us fix our eyes on Jesus, the author and perfecter of our faith'. Fixing our thoughts and our eyes on Jesus is incredibly practical and will help us see once again his central role in our Christian experience.

First a few introductory comments – there are two things we don't know about this letter. Firstly, we don't know who wrote it. If you have an Authorised Version it may say at the top of the page 'the Epistle of Paul the Apostle to the Hebrews'. Hebrews was certainly written in Paul's era but the book itself does not claim Pauline authorship and there are a number of reasons why we would seriously doubt that Paul was the writer. Number 1: he puts his name to all his other letters and there is no name of a writer in this epistle. Number 2: this author claims to be a second generation Christian. In 2:3 he speaks of 'This salvation, which was first announced by the Lord, was confirmed to us by those who heard him.' So the writer says, 'I'm second generation. There are folks who heard Jesus and they passed the gospel on to us.' If you read the letter to the Galatians, Paul specifically claims he did not receive the gospel message from any man; he received it directly from the Lord Jesus Christ himself. Number 3: the literary style is different to Paul's. On balance, therefore, it's extremely unlikely that Paul wrote this letter.

Secondly, we don't know who received it; we don't know whom it was specifically written for. We know it was written to a local church because it wasn't a general letter, as some of our New Testament letters are. In 13:23 the writer says, 'I want you to know that our brother Timothy has been released. If he arrives soon, I will come with him to see you.' So it's clearly written to a group of folks living in a specific geographical location. But the big question is, who were these folks? And the big answer is, we don't know. Again, there is a lot of speculation. But the title that we know this letter by, 'the letter to the Hebrews', has been known since the second century. It was probably not part of the original document but is most likely to be an accurate description. The consistent references to the Old Testament that run right through this letter presuppose a thorough familiarity with the Old Testament Scriptures and that strongly suggests that the author was writing to Jewish believers.

I'm going to assume that the epistle to the Hebrews is called the Epistle to the Hebrews because it's an epistle to the Hebrews. Is that a reasonable assumption? The Hebrews were the chosen people of God: God had set them apart as a nation. And when he called Abraham he said, 'I'll make you into a great nation and all peoples on earth will be blessed through you.' This promise, not just to set them apart as a distinct people, but, through them, to bless the world was dependent on the coming of a Messiah. The whole of Old Testament history, from Abraham on, orientates around the fact there's going to be a day when the anointed one of God, the Messiah, will step into our history. The prophets repeatedly looked beyond the immediate circumstances of the people they were addressing and said, 'But one day, one day there's going to come a Messiah.' Because until he came their destiny would remain unfilled. The tragedy is, as John explained, 'He came to that which was his own, but his own did not receive him' (Jn. 1:11). Why did they not receive him? Because they had misunderstood some fundamental things about him. So this letter to the Hebrews was written to address some of the fundamental misunderstandings about Jesus that the Jewish people had. The author is writing to correct their ignorance of who Christ was and to explain how Jesus Christ completes and fulfils Israel's history, Israel's law, Israel's ceremonial rituals and Israel's priesthood. These are some of the themes that run through this Letter. That's why Hebrews is the clearest exegesis of the Old Testament Scriptures that we have in the New Testament.

CHAPTER 1

The supremacy of Christ in revelation

Aim: To acknowledge Christ's supremacy in every area of life

FOCUS ON THE THEME
Share together examples of when you have clearly seen God's supremacy in your own life – a prayer answered, guidance given, the strength to persevere through hardship or a difficulty overcome.

Read: Hebrews 1:1–3:6
Key Verses: Hebrews 1:1-9, 3:1-6

The writer begins Hebrews 1:1 'In the past God spoke to our forefathers through the prophets at many times and in various ways, but in these last days he has spoken to us by his Son'. The writer takes one key thing for granted and that is that God speaks.

● *Share examples of the different ways that God has spoken to you.*

It's true that throughout history God has always spoken and the very first introduction we have to God, in Genesis 1, is of a God who speaks. Genesis begins 'In the beginning God ...' It doesn't explain him, doesn't prove him, just assumes him. And seven times in Genesis 1, it says 'and

God said, "Let there be light"... and God said, "Let there be an expanse between the waters", and God said ... and God said ... and God said.' If you know nothing else at the end of reading Genesis chapter 1, you know that God speaks. If God speaks it follows that he's got something to say that lies outside the realm of natural knowledge.

Psalm 19 tells us about the natural revelation of God, 'The heavens declare the glory of God; the skies proclaim the work of his hands. Day after day they pour forth speech; night after night they display knowledge. There is no speech or language where their voice is not heard. Their voice goes out into all the earth, their words to the ends of the world.' In other words, the Psalmist says, God speaks every night the stars come out. You look across the vastness of the universe and you say 'God is speaking about his greatness and his power.' Every time a little money spider runs across your table you say, 'God is speaking about his detail and his minute interests.' Creation reveals God. But if God speaks generally, he also speaks specifically. And, in these opening two and a half chapters of Hebrews, the writer talks about four key means by which God has spoken in the past and why these four key means are actually inadequate in themselves. In each of these four key areas, Christ becomes the superior revelation.

- *When is the last time you paused to notice God speaking through creation?*
- *What does creation tell us about God (Rom. 1:20)? What extra revelation about God did Christ bring?*

First of all, he is superior to the prophets (1:1-2). 'In the past God spoke to our forefathers through the prophets at many times and in various ways'. Amongst the Hebrews, of course, the prophets were the aristocracy of their history. The role of the prophet was very simple: it was to speak to people on God's behalf.

In Jeremiah 23 God says to the prophets of Israel, 'If you would only listen to me then you'd speak my word.' Because that was their job, to listen and speak. And they communicated God's message to people in various ways. They communicated through preaching; prefacing their message with 'Thus says the Lord'. They communicated through poetry. They communicated through music, for example in Isaiah 5 you've got the song of a vineyard. They communicated through drama. Ezekiel was a great actor; once he had to eat a scroll. For fifteen months he performed a one-man theatre show. Ezekiel had to draw a picture of Jerusalem on a clay board and then make some toy soldiers and some toy battering rams and get a frying pan, and then lie on his side with the pan between him and this model for three hundred and ninety days, thirteen months. And, after three hundred and ninety days he had to get up, turn over and lie on his right side for forty days, in front of the same model, to demonstrate that after three hundred and ninety years of Judah's rebellion, God was going to take them into exile for forty years of punishment.

God didn't just speak through drama, he also spoke through personal experience. The prophet Hosea was told to marry a woman called Gomer. Gomer became a prostitute and Hosea's heart was broken. God said, 'How do you feel about your wife?' Hosea's response, 'It hurts.' God said, 'That's what I feel about my people, they hurt.' In spite of the various ways God spoke, at the end of every prophecy, the prophet would go home, sit down, scratch his head and say, 'Something isn't right, something is missing from this.' We love the message of the prophets but in a moment we'll look at why Christ is superior to the prophets.

● *Rank the following in order of the most important way God speaks today:*
preaching/music/drama/poetry/personal experience.

● *If the supreme way God speaks is through Christ, what practices do we need to put into/take out of our lives to ensure we hear him clearly?*

● *Are there traditions or practices your church needs to change in order to hear Christ's voice more clearly?*

Secondly, Christ is superior to the priests. The priesthood is implied in the second part of 1:3, where the writer says that 'After he had provided purification for sins, he sat down at the right hand of the Majesty in heaven.' This theme of priesthood is developed more fully in chapters 5-10. The prophet and the priest were different because they had contrasting roles. The role of the prophet was to speak to people on God's behalf but the role of the priest was to speak to God on the people's behalf. God's message to people came through the prophets; man's appeal to God came through the priest.

The priesthood was based on blood sacrifices, an atonement to satisfy the just wrath of God. The primary function of the priest was to approach God for the purification of the sin of his people. But the problem with the priesthood, although God ordained it, was that the priest's work was never done. In 7:27, it says the priests 'offer sacrifices day after day, first for his own sins, then for the sins of the people.' It sounds tedious, doesn't it? It was a tedious role but here, in this verse, it speaks of Christ as the priest; when he provided purification for sins, he sat down. The priests of the old covenant never sat down. The priests had a vital role to play but at the end of every sacrifice, at the end of every day, down at the tabernacle or later in the Temple, the priest would go home, sit down, scratch his head and say, 'Something is missing, something isn't right here.' We love the message of the priests, they were ordained by God, but I'll tell you in a moment why Christ is superior to the priests.

● *Why was the priest's job never done? Why were the*
  animal sacrifices inadequate?

Thirdly, Christ is superior to the angels and this theme runs
from chapter 1:4–2:18. It says in 1:4, 'he became as much
superior to the angels as the name he has inherited is
superior to theirs.' And in 1:5-8 he quotes various Old
Testament passages where the Father addresses the Son in a
way he never addresses the angels. For example in 1:5-6, 'For
to which of the angels did God ever say, "You are my Son;
today I have become your Father"? Or again, "I will be his
Father and he will be my Son"?' 'Never,' says the writer, 'did
God ever say such things to angels that he says to Christ.'

The word angel literally means messenger. By definition
angels are messengers, that's their job, waiting for God to
give them instructions to carry messages. In fact, verse 14
calls them ministering spirits, 'Are not all angels
ministering spirits sent to serve those who will inherit
salvation?' They appear at various times in Scripture.
Seventeen times in the Old Testament there are angelic
visitations to individuals, couples or, on one occasion, to
the whole nation of Israel in the wilderness. In the New
Testament there are seven occasions when angels make
visitations, again to individuals or, on one occasion, to the
shepherds in Bethlehem at the time of the birth of Jesus.

Twenty-four times angels appear in Scripture and each
time the message they brought was binding. Chapter 2:2-3
says, 'For if the message spoken by angels was binding,
and every violation and disobedience received its just
punishment, how shall we escape if we ignore such a great
salvation?' The point is that an angel's message was
binding and every violation was punished. And then from
2:5-18 the writer talks about how Jesus Christ, becoming a
man, made himself a little lower than the angels. As a man
he was a little lower than the angels but 'now [he's]
crowned with glory and honour' (2:9). He's back in his

rightful place. The point of this whole section is that God has spoken through angels and we love the ministry of angels but it was not enough. I'll tell you, in a moment, why Christ is superior to the angels.

Fourthly, Christ is superior to Moses (3:1-6). Verses 3-6 says

> Jesus has been found worthy of greater honour than Moses, just as the builder of a house has greater honour than the house itself. For every house is built by someone, but God is the builder of everything. Moses was faithful as a servant in all God's house, testifying to what would be said in the future. But Christ is faithful as a son over God's house.

The writer makes the distinction that Moses was the servant whereas Christ was the Son. He singles out Moses for special mention because Moses had an unique place in the revelation that God gave to the Hebrew people. We're told in Exodus 33:11 'The Lord would speak to Moses face to face, as a man speaks with his friend.' It was to Moses that God revealed his law and the law of Moses becomes the plumb line, the chief legal authority in the history of the nation of Israel. Hebrews 10:28 reminds us 'Anyone who rejected the law of Moses died without mercy on the testimony of two or three witnesses.' And yet even Moses, being given the law which reveals the mind, character, and holiness of God, when he came down the mountain with the tablets of stone in his hand and gave them to the people of Israel, went back to his tent that night, sat down, scratched his head and said, 'This isn't enough, there's something missing.' I'll tell you, in a moment, why Christ is superior to Moses.

● *Like the Israelites, we often rely primarily on our church leaders rather than God. How do we find the balance*

*between following and obeying our leaders and
acknowledging that Christ is our supreme leader?*

Why is Christ superior to the prophets? To the priests? To
the angels? To Moses? Is it because Jesus Christ was a
better preacher than they were? Is it because Jesus Christ
had a better message than they did? Of course, in one
sense, that may be true but that is actually not the issue
being addressed here. Is it because he was more
trustworthy than these other messengers? Well no, we're
told the prophets were moved by the Holy Spirit and their
word was as authoritative as any word that came from the
lips of Jesus as they spoke under the movement and
inspiration of the Holy Spirit. They were men who spoke
from God. So why is Christ superior? Christ is superior
not because he was a better preacher, not because he had a
better message, not because he was more reliable but
because he himself is the message. He himself is the truth.

- *Look back over Hebrews 1:2-3. Pick out all the phrases
  referring to Christ. What do they tell us about him? How
  does this encourage/comfort you?*
- *Why do you think God left the best, Christ, until last?
  Why do you think God didn't put his best rescue plan into
  operation immediately but sent prophets, priests, angels
  and Moses to us first?*
- *Not many people would call Jesus' birth, death or lifestyle
  'superior'. What does this tell us about how God defines
  the term 'superior'? How do we need to change our values
  and priorities to be in line with his?*

FURTHER STUDY

Using a concordance, look up some of the accounts of angels speaking to individuals in the Old and New Testaments. From these conversations, what do you learn about God's concerns, priorities and his message to people?

Look at how prophets such as Jeremiah, Jonah, and Micah responded when God spoke to them. What lessons can we learn about how to respond to God – and how not to respond?

REFLECTION AND RESPONSE

As the writer to the Hebrews encouraged us, 'Holy brothers, who share in the heavenly calling, fix your thoughts on Jesus, the apostle and high priest whom we confess' (3:1). Use some of the phrases about the supremacy of Jesus to direct your prayers and choice of songs. Individually, take time to think what Christ's supremacy means to you. Acknowledge his supremacy in your:

- Problems at work
- Relationship struggles
- Financial worries
- Health concerns

If it is appropriate, share and pray through issues together in twos.

CHAPTER 2

Jesus is the truth

Aim: To examine the implications of Jesus being the truth

FOCUS ON THE THEME
 A fun quiz to test how truthful you are:
- Have you ever lied about your age or weight?
- Have you ever embellished your CV to try and get a job?
- Have you ever lied to a policeman to avoid a speeding fine?
- Have you ever lied when a friend asked if you liked their new outfit?
- Have you lied in these questions?

Even if we consider ourselves basically truthful, we have probably told a few white lies. Can you begin to imagine what it means that Jesus not only told the truth and acted in truth but is the absolute truth?

Read: Hebrews 1:1–3:6
Key verse: Hebrews 1:1

The message that came through the prophets, through the priests, through the angels and through Moses was all true but it was not the truth. Remember Jesus, in the upper room, said, 'I am the truth'. John 14:6 records Jesus saying 'I am the way and the truth.' These previous messengers spoke truth but Jesus was the truth. Perhaps you travel frequently by train? You may have a timetable that tells you a train will leave Penrith station at ten o'clock on Saturday morning and arrive in Euston at two fifteen. That may be true, and if you're planning to catch that train, you hope it is – but the timetable, although it's true, is not the truth. The timetable bears witness to the truth. What is the truth? The truth is the train. A timetable won't get you anywhere. You can sit in your hotel room and you can read the timetable, underline it, memorise it, sing it: it won't get you anywhere. It's true but it's true only in the sense it bears witness to the truth, which is the train. That's the truth, that's what the timetable is talking about. God's revelation through the prophets, through the priests, through angels, through Moses is true but it's like the timetable, which is pointing to a train.

- *How did the prophets, priests, angels and Moses bear witness to Jesus, in what ways did they point to his coming?*

I could paraphrase Hebrews 1:1 'In the past God spoke to our forefathers through the timetables at many times and in various ways, but in these last days he's given us the train.' Does that make sense? Everything that went before, pointed to Christ, it didn't take you anywhere. The priests could tell the people there was somewhere to go but they could not take them because the message of the Old Testament is that one day the train is going to pull into the station. But the problem is that when the train came they did not receive him; they did not catch the train.

- *Why did people not recognise Jesus as the one they'd been waiting for?*
- *Why do people not recognise who Jesus is today?*
- *What will happen to the people who lived and died before Jesus came, who did not have the opportunity to know the truth?*

In Hebrews 10:1 the writer says 'The law is only a shadow of the good things that are coming – not the realities themselves.' There's nothing wrong with the law at all but it's only the shadow, it's not the substance; it's the timetable, it's not the train. It won't get you anywhere as Hebrews 10:1 explains: 'For this reason it can never, by the same sacrifices repeated endlessly year after year, make perfect those who draw near to worship.' Was it a waste of time? No, it was preparing people for what was coming. 10:11 says 'Day after day every priest stands and performs his religious duties; again and again he offers the same sacrifices, which can never take away sins.' So why does he carry on doing it? Because this is the timetable that foreshadows and explains the train. One day the train will come.

Jesus Christ is himself the truth. That's why the teaching of Jesus sets him apart from any other religious leader who ever lived, because his teaching was centred on himself: he was self-centred in his teaching. Other religious leaders have said things like, 'I will show you the way.' What did Jesus say? 'I am the way.' It's a very big difference. Others said, 'I will teach you the truth.' He said, 'I am the truth.' Others said, 'I will give you the life.' He said, 'I am the life.' Others said, 'I will feed you the bread.' He said, 'I am the bread of life.' Others have said, ' I will give you shepherds.' He said, 'I am the good shepherd.' Others have said, 'I will open the door for you.' Jesus said, 'I am the door.' Others have said, 'I will switch on the light.' Jesus said, 'I am the light.' Others have said, 'Go to Mecca, go to the Ganges.' What did Jesus say? 'Come to me.'

This letter to the Hebrews has been written to a group of Hebrew believers in a particular historical, cultural setting. They have become so wrapped up in the timetable, in all the true things God had revealed through his agents in the past in many ways at various times. But they'd missed the truth to which it all pointed and on which it all centred: Christ himself. The popular, standard world view today is that there is no truth. When there is no truth there are only opinions and if there are only opinions your opinion is as valid as mine and mine is no more valid than yours. You find that most discussions you may have with other folks about Christ will simply be a discussion of one opinion against another. The idea that there's truth is alien to much of our thinking. You measure the benefit of any religion by the good it does for its followers, not whether it's true or not.

● *How can we do evangelism well in our generation? How can we present Jesus as the truth to people who do not believe in absolute truth?*

I heard a minister several years ago say, 'Jesus Christ is the Christians' truth, he is our truth. But we dare not say he is the only truth, that he is the Muslims' truth.' Afterwards, I said to him, 'I was interested in your comments today. Do you think Jesus knew what he was talking about?' He said, 'What's behind your question?' I said, 'Jesus said "I am the truth. I am the way, I am the truth, the life, no one comes to the Father but by me."' I said, 'Do you think the apostles were trustworthy? Peter said, in Acts 4:12, "Salvation is found in no-one else, for there is no other name under heaven given to men by which we must be saved."'

What would you say in the following scenarios:
● *You were explaining the Christian faith to a friend and they say 'I feel uncomfortable about a faith that is not so much about a philosophy or a way of life as about a person, a person who wants my total allegiance and adoration. That strikes me as selfish.'*
● *One of your Christian friends says 'All truth is God's truth' so feels free to practice reflexology. Another friend thinks she shouldn't be involved in practices that have associations with New Age.*

- *Your boss asks you not to mention that you are a Christian because he doesn't want to offend those of other faiths who work in the office.*
- *A Christian friend tells you they don't like sharing their faith because it seems offensive to say to people that Jesus is the truth; the only way to God.*

Jesus Christ is superior to all that preceded him, not because what he said was better, not because what he said was more complete, though it was. It's far more fundamental than that, it's because Christ himself is the message and he has absolutely unmatched supremacy in God's revelation. That's why you should 'fix your thoughts on Jesus, fix your eyes on Jesus', because you decapitate truth when you sever it from Christ. If you detach the Scripture from Christ, the Scripture becomes a dead book. It's still inspired but it's a dead book.

I was on a flight one day, going from London to Los Angeles, and, as we left London, I was sitting next to a man in his mid-twenties. At one point, I pulled my Bible out and began to read it and this young man turned to me and said, 'It's nice to see somebody reading their Bible.' I said, 'It's nice to meet somebody who thinks it's nice to see somebody reading their Bible.' So I said the obvious thing to him, 'Are you a Christian?' He said, 'I would say I am but you probably would say I'm not.' I said, 'Really, why is that?' He said, 'Because I'm a Christadelphian.' Many of you will know the Christadelphian sect. They deny the deity of Christ, the personality of the Holy Spirit and other fundamentals. So I said, 'You're right, I would say you're not a Christian, on these grounds, "No one comes to the Father but by me" and if you don't understand Christ correctly as "the way", you close off the only access we have to God.'

He stood up and pulled out his briefcase from the compartment above, got out an old King James

Authorised Version of the Bible, it had been his grandfather's. He opened this Bible, it had pen marks and colours on every page and this young man, impressively, knew his Bible. I had my Bible in my hand, he had his Bible in his hand and we ran around our various Bibles. He'd jump into Hebrews, find a rabbit hole, disappear, reappear in Leviticus, go into Deuteronomy, find another one, reappear in Revelation. He was back, forth, with markings on every page but the tragedy was, it was a dead book in his hand. It was still the inspired word of God in its origin but it was dead in his hand. Why? He had detached Scripture from Christ and if you detach Scripture from Christ, it's a dead book. That's exactly what the Jews did. That's why Jesus actually criticised them for studying the Bible. In John 5:39-40 he said 'You diligently study the Scriptures because you think that by them you possess eternal life.' But 'These are the Scriptures that testify about me, yet you refuse to come to me to have life.' So these Jews studied the Scriptures, thought they had eternal life, thought they had the secret and what does it do? It made them into Pharisees, because it gave them a book of laws to hit everybody over the head with.

I used to have a Toyota Carina car. When I bought that Toyota Carina I got with it an instruction book. I read the instruction book and the reason I read the instruction book was not because I wanted to know all about the instruction book. I had a far better reason; I wanted to know all about the car. I could have read the instruction book to get to know the instruction book. I could have read a little bit, every night, before I went to bed, I could have underlined the bits that I liked, I could have joined the local Toyota fellowship and gone every week for an exposition of the manual. 'This week's subject is sparking gloves, next week we're going to have a message on tyre pressures.' I could have put it to music and sung it. If I was a fanatic, I could have studied

Japanese to read it in the original language, that would really impress everyone. But the day would come, having read the manual, memorised it, underlined it, put it to music and sung it and studied Japanese, the day would come when I would say, 'I'm sick of the manual.' Why? Because the manual has one purpose, to take me to the car. When Jesus criticised the Jews for studying the Scriptures, he wasn't undermining the authority or the inspiration or the integrity of the word of God. He was simply explaining, it's not the truth. It's true because it points to the truth. That's why you can study the Bible and get a degree in theology and know nothing of spiritual reality. Remember that old hymn *Break thou the bread of life* which has the great line, 'Beyond the sacred page I seek thee, Lord'. From Genesis to Revelation, every verse leads to Christ, ultimately. And it's knowing him, the truth, that really matters.

- *Your quiet times are in a rut; they're dry and feel like an academic exercise. How can you revive these times so that they are opportunities to meet Jesus and get to know him better?*

- *'Every verse leads to Christ, ultimately'. What does that mean? How should we be reading and studying our Bibles so that we see Christ in every verse?*

FURTHER STUDY
Scan through one of the gospels for the occasions when Jesus says 'truly, truly'. If Jesus, the truth, says 'truly, truly', what follows must be important. Are there any particular commands or encouragements that you need to take to heart?

REFLECTION AND RESPONSE
The media shapes our worldview more than we realise. Newspapers, magazines and TV programmes shape how we think about ourselves

and others. But Jesus is the truth so it is his thoughts and perspective we should rely on for our values and outlook on life. Brainstorm verses from the Bible that say:

• What Jesus thinks about you
• What key things he wants you to do for him
• What truths he wants you to base your life on

Write some of these verses down to encourage you. Pray for each other this week that you would meet with Jesus in your devotional times and you'd get to know him better. When you next meet, share what God has been teaching you.

CHAPTER 3

Real God, real humanity

Aim: To learn the truth Jesus teaches us about God and ourselves

FOCUS ON THE THEME
Who have been the great teachers in your life? Why were they so good? Why did they make such an impact? To what extent do these other teachers match up to Jesus? What makes him a good teacher of the truth?

Read: Hebrews 1:1–3:6
Key verse: Hebrews 1:3

If Jesus Christ is the truth, what is he the truth about? He's the truth about two things. First of all he's the truth about God. Jesus teaches us what God is like. In verse 3 it says 'The Son is the radiance of God's glory and the exact representation of his being, sustaining all things by his powerful word.' In other words, if you want to know what God is like, look at Jesus. God is nothing that Jesus isn't or, to put it positively, everything Jesus is, God is. He's the exact representation of God. That's why we don't know God propositionally, by simply learning facts about him. We can say that God is omnipotent; he's all-powerful. God is omnipresent; he's everywhere at the same time. He is omniscient; he knows everything there is to know. God is eternal; he has no beginning and no end. We can learn these propositional truths but they won't make us love him. They'll make us respect him but they won't make us excited by him. It's when you know Christ that you begin to love him.

● *Why do people find it difficult to accept the truth that Jesus is the exact representation of God?*

The Christian life is saying with Paul in 2 Timothy 1:12, 'I know whom I have believed'. It is not saying 'I know *what* I have believed.' Knowing what you believe is fine, signing your name with a good conscience at the end of the creed is fine but the Christian life is about knowing whom I have believed. The more you know Jesus, the more you know God and the more you love Jesus, the more you love God and the more you trust Jesus, the more you trust God. In fact, it's only when we know Christ that we know God. Jesus Christ is the truth about God, the exact representation of his being.

● *Explain why is it by knowing Christ that we come to know God.*

● *A local minister is frustrated that his congregation of Christians know a lot more since he started preaching but they haven't recovered any of the fervour they had when they first became Christians. Is he justified? What would you say to him?*

● *Knowing Jesus helps us know God. What have been the most effective ways you have got to know Jesus better? Was it through*
  – A small group
  – Challenging preaching
  – Your own devotional time
  – Good role models
  – Other

Secondly, Jesus is the truth about humanity; he teaches us what humanity should be like. When the writer says, 'The

Son is the radiance of God's glory and the exact representation of his being,' he is not only speaking about his deity, he is actually, remarkably, speaking about his humanity. Just as Jesus is the representation of God, so is Adam. What did God say when he created Adam? 'Let us make man in our image, in our likeness.' Theologians have debated what it means for us to be made in the image of God. We know there are things in God that are not true of man. For example, God is omnipresent; we're not. So in what sense were we made in his image? I suggest to you that we were created in his moral image. God is love and we are intended to be loving. God is kind and we are created to be an expression of his moral image. If you want to know what God was like in the Garden of Eden, look at Adam; if you want to know what God is like now, look at Jesus. Jesus is the truth about humanity and what God intended humanity to be.

Human beings were created to portray the truth about God. Adam was created to be a revelation of God. If you look at Adam, you see what God is like. Adam would be very kind because God is kind. The way Adam treated Eve, the way they handled the animals in the Garden, the way they patted the dog, stroked the cat and fed the goldfish, show us what God is like. Because when you look at an image, you see what the real thing is like. But Adam came short of the glory of God, he sinned and ceased to show us what God was like. But in Jesus we have the truth about what human beings were intended to be, when God created them in the first place. In 1 Corinthians Paul calls Jesus the 'second man', the 'last Adam' because he truly was the radiance of God's glory. If you want to know what you're supposed to be like, look at Jesus. He's the truth about humanity. We were created to be a physical and visible expression of the moral character of God.

● *Think back over the past week. When have your actions not portrayed the truth about God? Share occasions when your character has not reflected God's.*

● *As church bodies we were created to be expressions of God. What perception does your local community have of your church? What more could you do to reflect Christ in your locality?*

But the marvellous thing is, not only is Christ himself the radiance of God's glory, but bringing God's glory to earth was the object of his work and his ministry. In Hebrews 2:10 it speaks of him 'In bringing many sons to glory, it was fitting that God, for whom and through whom everything exists, should make the author of their salvation perfect through suffering.' And, by the way, don't misread that, that doesn't mean 'in bringing many sons to heaven.' In evangelical slang, basically the word 'glory' has come to mean heaven; we say 'we die and go to glory.' That's not the biblical use of the word. Glory is the character of God.

John says, of Jesus, 'The Word became flesh, lived for a while among us. We saw his glory.' What did he see? We saw in Jesus the way, as a boy, he kicked his ball up and down the road in Nazareth, the way he went hunting in the hills with his friends, hiding in the woods. The way, as a carpenter, he paid his bills on time, invoiced accurately and on time, built someone's kitchen furniture to their specification. The way, in his public ministry, he crossed the road to sit with a dirty woman everybody else was embarrassed to be seen with. The way he touched the untouchables, the lepers. Have you ever noticed Jesus always touched lepers? The way kids would climb all over him and the disciples would try to shoo them away and he'd say, 'No, no, let them come, they're my friends.' In Jesus, we saw what God was like, we saw the character of God, we saw the glory of God.

Because we're in the situation where we've sinned, come short of the glory of God, we don't show what God is like any more. We've become selfish and live for our own agendas. But now, in Jesus, we see not only the glory of God but we see one whose goal is to bring many sons to glory, to put back what was lost in the fall. That's why Colossians 1:27 says 'Christ in you, the hope of glory.' Jesus is going to bring you back to glory. We're going to see how this God, who became a man, can restore us to glory and put back what was lost. The Scriptures are true but it's Christ who's the truth; it's he who by his indwelling presence in your life makes this faith journey real. It was foreshadowed in the times of the prophets but now in Christ we see clearly how to come home, how to be what God intended human beings to be.

- *In what particular aspect of your life do you want Christ to restore the glory? Is there a sin you keep on committing, an aspect of your past you need to let go of or a person you need to forgive?*

- *What account in the life of Christ shows him living out the character trait you most need to emulate? Meditate and draw strength from these Scripture verses during the week.*

- *What barriers are you putting in the way of the Holy Spirit? Are you doing anything to hinder the Spirit's work of making you more like Christ and restoring you to glory?*

- *Jesus was fully human yet sometimes we struggle to admit our own humanness. What aspects of your humanity do you struggle with? What aspects of humanity does the church struggle with?*

FURTHER STUDY

Read through one of the Gospels. Take note of Jesus' actions, attitudes and behaviour – what does he teach us about what humanity should be like? What lessons can we learn from Jesus' example? Be specific.

REFLECTION AND RESPONSE

Jesus teaches us the truth about God and humanity. He's a good teacher because he not only spoke the truth but he demonstrated it for us: he lived on earth 100 per cent God, 100 per cent man. Jesus is a good teacher but how good a student are you? Think back over the past year or six months, what lessons have you learnt?

- How much better do you know God?
- To what extent are you living as God intended?
- How much more glory has been restored in your life?

Reflect on what Jesus wants to teach you in this phase of your life and be obedient.

As you consider your role as a student, remember that you are also a teacher. What are your words and example teaching others? Is there a younger Christian you could befriend or mentor, teaching them the truth about God and humanity?

REVIEW OF HEBREWS 1:1–3:6

Jesus Christ is supreme. He is supreme over all creation; he is the ultimate truth about God and man. The prophets, priests, angels and Moses had their value but Jesus is God's ultimate word to us. The Israelites needed mediators and an elaborate sacrificial system to meet God, but through Christ we have immediate access to the Father. Sometimes we forget how privileged we are: we enter God's presence carelessly and we take our relationship with God the Son too casually. Sometimes we treat Christ as a mate rather than the Supreme Lord of All.

Spend time worshipping Christ for his supremacy. Appreciate again what it cost for us to come freely into God's presence. In the quietness, consider what Christ's supremacy in your life really means:

- Are there areas of your life you need to surrender to his control?
- Are their areas of your life you have got to trust to his sovereignty?

Give thanks that Christ is in control of the big picture in a way that we could never understand and is still completely trustworthy with the minutiae of our personal lives.

POINTS TO PONDER
- What have you learnt about God?
- What have you learnt about yourself?
- What actions or attitudes do you need to change as a result?

CHAPTER 4

Heaven-filled hearts

Aim: To examine the condition of our hearts

FOCUS ON THE THEME
When you've been a Christian a short while, you soon learn how you are supposed to behave and the accepted formula of words. Imagine you are a church leader wanting to get beyond the surface piety of your congregation to discover what their relationship with God is really like. How would you go about this? What measures could you use to gauge people's hearts toward God? The number of people who turn up to the prayer meeting, the number of people who offer hospitality after the church service, or those who care for the poor...?

Read: Hebrews 3:7- 4:13
Key verses: Hebrews 3:7-4:2

You may have heard the story of the elderly husband who became convinced that his wife was losing her hearing. This became a rather sensitive subject because she was convinced she wasn't. The situation seemed to get worse and worse until, one day, the husband decided to do a little experiment. His wife was sitting in the lounge, he was in the kitchen and he said, 'Would you like a cup of tea, dear?' There was no response, which is what he'd expected. So he went into the passageway between the two rooms and said again, 'Would you like a cup of tea, dear? There was no response. Well, that didn't surprise him so he crept into the lounge, stood right behind her chair and said, 'Would you like a cup of tea, dear?' And she said, 'For the third time, yes.'

Maybe some of you are aware that something is not right in your walk with God. Maybe you've wondered 'where was that blessedness I knew, when first I saw the Lord?' You might blame your church, that's an easy target. You might blame your spouse; you might think your children are the reason you find it difficult to be close to God. Or it could be that the problem is yours? In this passage the writer of Hebrews gives the first of five warnings to his readers. He wants them to see their personal responsibility to be obedient and respond to God.

● *Draw a diagram to describe your walk with God at the moment. You could be on a plateau, going round in circles, on a sharp decline or a gradual incline. If it is appropriate, explain the reasoning behind your diagram to the group.*

To understand this passage we need to go back to the Old Testament. The author of Hebrews is retelling the well-known Exodus story that the Jewish Christians would have been very familiar with. The Exodus was the most glorious event in Israel's history, when God intervened, delivered and liberated them from their years of slavery and bondage in a foreign land. But it was also one of the most disastrous events in their history when they spent forty years in a wilderness going nowhere and doing nothing. To borrow from Dickens, 'it was the best of times and it was the worst of times.'

God had wonderfully intervened in Israel's affairs; they had been in Egypt for four hundred years. They'd arrived, originally just seventy-two of them, as honoured guests, relatives of Joseph who had been the saviour of Egypt during seven years of famine. His family and all their children had come to join him there. They had been welcomed, they were given some of the choice land in the Nile Delta, the Goshen area. Then they stayed and began to multiply until they became a threat to the Egyptians. Four hundred years later there were at least two million of them – six hundred thousand fighting men plus their wives and children – that came to leave Egypt.

God intervened by calling, equipping and sending Moses, and Moses led them out of Egypt. The writer of Hebrews retells this Exodus story because he sees here a parallel to the work of Christ and a parallel to our Christian experience. He introduces us to a literary aspect of the New Testament and particularly of Hebrews that we call 'typology'. That is where events in history become types or pictures that foreshadow Christ. The story that gets the most exposure in the whole of the Bible, Old and New Testaments, is the story of the Israelites coming out of Egypt, going through the wilderness and arriving in Canaan. And the reason why it has so much exposure is it's full of typology, full of pictures of the Christian life.

● *What modern day typology could you use to explain the gospel to:*
   – An unchurched colleague
   – A teenager who was into New Age thinking
   – A tradesman working in your home

Egypt is portrayed as slavery to sin, you read that in the book of Jude; the Passover lamb is a beautiful picture of Jesus. When John the Baptist introduced Jesus to the world by the Jordan River, he said, 'Behold the lamb of God who takes away the sin of the world.' Every Jew knew exactly what John was talking about because every year they re-enacted the Passover and John said, 'This is the Passover lamb.' Paul says, 'Christ, our Passover, was sacrificed for us.' The Exodus, the actual deliverance, is a picture of deliverance from sin. In fact the death of Christ is called, at his transfiguration, his Exodus. Crossing the Red Sea is also a picture of baptism. As Paul tells the Corinthians, 'we're all baptised into Moses in the Red Sea.' Why? Because they left their old master dead and buried in the Red Sea. Baptism is a picture of death to the old life and resurrection to new life.

When the Israelites crossed the Red Sea and were in the desert there was no water and so God said to Moses, 'Take your staff and strike the rock.' And water came out of the rock and that rock accompanied them, we're told. Paul says that rock was Christ. The rock from which they drew the water to satisfy their thirst was a picture of Christ. They ran out of food, God fed them manna. And, in a discussion in John 6 when the Jews said, 'Our forefathers fed us with bread in the wilderness', Jesus corrected them. 'It wasn't your forefathers at all, it was my Father who fed you with bread.' Then he said, 'I am the true bread.'

Canaan, the land to which the Hebrews went, is portrayed here in chapter 4 as 'resting in the fullness of God', with all the resources we need to accomplish the task for which he saved us. Canaan is resting in Christ and enjoying the fullness of his presence in our lives. But the reason the writer retells the Exodus story here is because God has spoken and some of us are not listening. Do you know what happens when you don't listen? You may be saved but you get stuck. The writer focuses on the forty years Israel spent in the wilderness because the journey from Egypt to Canaan should have only lasted eleven days. Deuteronomy 1:2 says 'It takes eleven days to go from Horeb (Horeb was where Moses met God in the burning bush) to Kadesh Barnea'. It's less than three hundred miles on the map. It took them forty years; it should have taken eleven days. We often get stuck in our Christian lives and, like the Israelites, make little or no progress and seem to go round in circles. To find out what God really had in mind for us, we need to go back to basics and look at the purpose of the Exodus.

- *What would have been comfortable about the wilderness existence for the Israelites?*
- *What makes us comfortable in our own wildernesses? What stops us getting to Canaan?*

The reason God delivered Israel from Egypt is not because he felt sorry for them in their slavery. It wasn't to make life easy for Israel; it wasn't to get the taskmasters off their backs so they no longer had to listen to the crack of the whip every morning. God's purpose was to bring them out of Egypt in order to bring them into Canaan, a land he described as flowing with milk and honey, where they would fulfil their destiny and from where they would, as he had already told Abraham, bless the world. God reiterated that when he called Moses at the burning bush. Exodus 3:8 records God's words, 'I have come down to rescue them from the hand of the Egyptians and to bring them up out of that land into a good and spacious land, a land flowing with milk and honey'. In other words, coming out of Egypt was not the end in itself. When the Israelites crossed the Red Sea, God didn't stroke his brow and say 'Phew, they're out, wonderful, that's it.' They came out of Egypt in order to come into Canaan, that, from there, they might bless the world.

Many times in the wilderness God reminded the Hebrews of his purpose – 'I am the Lord your God, who brought you out of Egypt to give you the land of Canaan and to be your God' (Lev. 25:38). But they were stuck in the wilderness and God said 'I brought you out to bring you in.' So what went wrong? In Deuteronomy 6:23 Moses says, 'He brought us out from there to bring us in and to give us the land that he promised on oath to our forefathers.' In other words, God's plan wasn't anything new; it was re-establishing the original purpose for which he had set Israel apart, that from that land they'd bless the world. But they failed to enter in.

Let me just pause and ask the question, 'Why did God save you?' Was it because he felt sorry for you? Did God save you and me in order to ease our guilty consciences? Did he save us so we might be forgiven? Did he save us so we might go to heaven instead of hell? These are wonderful aspects of the gospel. But in all the New Testament, in the preaching of Jesus, in the preaching of the apostles – and we have nineteen messages or fragments of messages in the books of Acts – eight by Peter, nine by Paul, one by Stephen, one by Philip, going to heaven was never once the reason for becoming a Christian. It was a consequence but it's never the reason. So what's the reason? Look at Paul praying for the Ephesians in 3:14

> For this reason I kneel before the Father, from whom his whole family in heaven and on earth derives its name. I pray that out of his glorious riches he may strengthen you with power through his Spirit in your inner being, so that Christ may dwell in your hearts through faith. And I pray that you, being rooted and established in love, may have power, together with all the saints, to grasp how wide and long and high and deep is the love of Christ, and to know this love that surpasses knowledge – that you may be filled to the measure of all the fullness of God.

'I'm praying these things for you,' says Paul, 'in order that your Christian life will go on getting deeper, your knowledge of God higher, deeper, wider, that you may know his fullness.' That's Ephesians 3. In Ephesians 4 Paul gives a list of some of the gifts God's given to the church.

And in verse 13 he explains the goal – 'until we all reach unity in the faith and in the knowledge of the Son of God and become mature'. What's maturity? Maturity is 'attaining to the whole measure of the fulness of Christ.' So, what Paul says in this letter to the Ephesians is that the end product of your Christian life is that you're filled with the fullness of God. The reason why God gives ministries and gifts to the church is so that we may know the stature of the fullness of Christ (Eph. 4). The will of God is that you're 'filled with the Spirit' (Eph. 5:18). That's not three fullnesses of course; filled with God, filled with Christ, and filled with the Spirit. It is the fullness of the Godhead.

What's the goal of the Christian life? It's not primarily to get us out of hell and into heaven. It is primarily to get God out of heaven and into people. Then God himself, once again, reigns in the hearts of men and women, boys and girls, and fills them with himself. But we can be so excited about coming out that we fail to fulfil the purpose to go in. The reasons the Israelites failed to come into Canaan and the reasons we fail to progress towards maturity may be the same – that's why the author of Hebrews makes this comparison.

The reason the Israelites didn't go into Canaan was because of hardened hearts. Hebrews 3:7 reminds us, 'Today, if you hear his voice, do not harden your hearts'. In Hebrews 3:10 God says 'That is why I was angry with that generation, and I said, "Their hearts are always going astray"'. Disobedience begins as a hardened heart and becomes a wayward heart. In verse 15 he says, 'As has just been said: "Today, if you hear his voice, do not harden your hearts as you did in the rebellion."' Some translations speak of an 'unbelieving heart', the NIV speaks of a 'hardened heart'. Whatever the translation, the problem is the heart. What does it mean to have a hardened heart? To have a wayward heart? To have an unbelieving heart?

Chapter 4:2 explains to us what happened to the Israelites' hearts. The writer reminds the Hebrews, 'we also have had the gospel preached to us, just as they did'. Of course, we recognise the gospel the Israelites had preached to them was different in substance to the gospel that we have had preached to us but it's the same in principle. God had something good for them; God had something good for us too. So we've had the gospel preached to us as they had the gospel preached to them, 'but the message they heard was of no value to them'. It didn't do them any good. Why not? 'Because those who heard did not combine it with faith.' You may be a Christian, your sins have been forgiven, you've received that gift of eternal life but there are resources that you've never tapped into. There are purposes you've never connected with. Why? 'Because those who heard did not combine it with faith.' Truth, in itself, doesn't do you any good unless it's combined with faith. The Authorised Version says 'mixed with faith'. If you detach truth from faith, it's of no value.

- *How does hardening of the heart start? Look at Hebrews 3:7,10,13 as well as brainstorming your own ideas.*
- *What steps can you take if you feel far away from God and know your heart is beginning to harden?*
- *Hebrews 3:13 tells us to encourage one another. What role can encouragement play in keeping our hearts receptive toward God? In what formal and informal ways can encouragement take place among Christians?*
- *Share examples of occasions you have been impressed by individuals combining truth and faith; times when people have known God's truth and lived it out in dependency on him, perhaps in adverse situations.*

FURTHER STUDY

Look up in a concordance some of the times the word 'heart' is used. The heart isn't just an organ pumping blood around the body: what is the term 'heart' shorthand for?

REFLECTION AND RESPONSE

The goal of salvation is being filled with all the fullness of God. What is stopping God from filling you completely?

• Are you not spending enough time with him?

• Is there a sin you enjoy indulging?

• Are you resisting his lordship in some area of your life?

Confess the condition of your heart before God and invite him to keep on filling you with his fullness.

Discuss the concerns of the coming week with one other person in the group and pray together that you would both keep pressing on to Canaan, knowing that God has provided all the resources you need for the tasks he has given.

CHAPTER 5

What is faith?

Aim: Learning to allow God to work on our behalf

FOCUS ON THE THEME
Look through this week's newspapers and popular magazines. What do the articles and adverts reveal about who and what our generation put their faith in? To what extent do you put your faith in the same things?

Read: Hebrews 3:7–4:13
Key verses: Hebrews 3:7-19

Now what is faith? Faith is one of the most misunderstood words in the Christian vocabulary. The whole of our Christian life operates on the basis of faith. But what is it? Let me define it negatively first of all and say what faith isn't. There are those who have the idea that faith is some kind of mystical power: if you close your eyes and really, really believe something strongly enough, you'll make it happen.

I remember when I used to work at Capernwray, an international Bible school in North Lancashire. During one of the summer conferences I was going down to the conference hall for the morning session and it was a typical, North Lancashire summer's day: it was raining. I caught up with a man and his wife walking under a huge golf umbrella and said, 'Do you mind if I walk with you?' I joined them and then said, 'It's going to be a miserable day today, isn't it?' The lady turned to me, 'Don't say that.' I said, 'Why not?' She replied, 'You should say it's going to be a beautiful day today.' I said, 'But it isn't, it's going to be a miserable day. It's been raining all night, it's raining now, the clouds are thick, the forecast says it'll rain all day, if not all week, probably all month, probably all summer.' She said, 'But you should say, "It's going to be a beautiful day, the clouds will blow away, the sun will come out, we'll all get a sun tan."' I said, 'Why?' She said, 'That's faith.' That isn't faith, that's actually stupidity. You can stand in a rainstorm, believe what you like, the rain will take no notice. I know some Christians who are almost having nervous breakdowns trying to believe black is white.

- *What is wrong with the view that faith is believing something strongly enough to make it happen?*
- *Share examples of occasions you have seen this definition of faith in operation.*

Other folks have the idea that faith is what you need when you run out of facts. As long as you've got your facts you're secure but when you get to the end of your facts, 'Uh oh.' This is where you need faith. Faith is believing what you can't prove, it's a leap into the dark, it's hoping something's true and you're in luck. Well, of course, we believe things we can't prove in an objective, scientific manner. You can't say to your neighbour, 'Here's the evidence for God: this multiplied by this, divided by that, plus this, squared by that equals God.' As a definition of faith, it's wholly inadequate. Faith is not a substitute for facts, for the simple reason facts are necessary for the exercise of faith. Faith has to be in an object, it has to be *in* something. You can't just have faith on its own, any more than you can just have love on its own.

Imagine you met a teenage girl whose knees were knocking and whose eyes were rolling, who was giddy and off her food and you say, 'What's the matter with you?' She replies, 'I'm all in love.' And you ask 'Who are you in love with?' 'Nobody, I'm just in love.' You can't be in love with nobody. You've got to love an object. It might be a cat, a teddy bear, a car or a person. The all-important thing about your love is the object; so it is with faith. Faith only exists in relationship to an object because faith has to be in something and it is the object in which you place your faith that determines the validity of it. Your faith is no more valid than the object in which it is placed.

Let me illustrate: if I put a lot of faith in some thin ice, with all the faith in the world, if I step onto the thin ice – what do you think is going to happen? I'll sink, by faith. Now what's my problem? Is it my faith? No, it's the ice. On the other hand, if I put a little bit of faith in some thick ice and, very nervously, with a life belt around my waist, some rope tied to the nearest tree, and a note written to my wife saying 'Goodbye, if I don't come home I'm under the ice', if with my little bit of faith, I step on to the thick ice, what do you think will happen? I'll walk on the ice because I had more faith? No, I might have had a little bit of faith but the object in which I placed my faith was stronger.

- *Be honest and come up with a list of things you are trusting in. Perhaps you're trusting in your health, money or spouse. To what extent is it appropriate to trust these things? How reliable are they?*
- *What stops you putting your faith/trust in God alone?*
- *Consider a specific situation you are trusting God in. What difference does it make to remember that it is not the amount of faith you have but the object in which you place your faith that counts?*

Faith is a disposition of trust in an object for the purpose of allowing that object to work on my behalf. You're exercising faith right now as you sit on your seat. You put your faith in the chair and you allowed your body to come crashing down and land on it. And, right now, you're bent at the knees and bent at the middle. What's holding you in that position? Although you sat down as an act of faith, what's holding you in that position is not your faith, what's holding you is the chair in which you placed your faith. Is that right? If you're not sure do an experiment but make sure nobody's watching because it might be embarrassing. Take away the chair and sit on your faith. Do you know what you'll discover? You'll discover that your faith is totally meaningless unless it's placed in an object for the purpose of allowing the object to work on your behalf. You're not doing anything for the chair; you're letting the chair do something for you.

You put faith in a car, what does that mean? You let the car take you down the road, you don't do anything for the car, you can go to sleep on the back seat, but it's the car doing something for you. You put faith in an aircraft, what does that mean? You let the aircraft do something for you, you do nothing for the aircraft, you just sit down, relax, read a book, and the aircraft will fly you through the air. So what is faith in God? It's letting God do something, it's letting God work.

Consider the following scenarios:

- *A young boy in the church has been diagnosed with severe asthma. His mother will not acknowledge or treat the condition but says that her faith in God will make her son well. What would you say to her? What is wrong with her concept of faith?*

- *A friend of yours heard a preacher say you need to claim by faith what you want, whether it's a husband, new house or new job. How would you respond?*

- *A childless couple is told by another member of the congregation that they just need to have faith if they want a baby. They are understandably upset. How would you comfort them? What does having faith in their situation really mean?*

● *Why are we so tempted to view faith as something we do rather than as letting God do something for us?*

Now, in their release from Egypt, the Hebrews had ample evidence of God's utter sufficiency and his work on their behalf. He had worked by releasing them, by opening the Red Sea, bringing them through on dry ground. If you're a Christian, today, you already have had experience of a God who's intervened in your life, cleansed you, forgiven you, and placed his Holy Spirit in you. But the tragedy is, having been saved by faith, the Israelites then tried to live by human effort and live, simply, by human disciplines. They became detached from dependency on God, for the purpose that God might work in their situation.

Sometimes, we get the idea that the work of God, having saved us, is to give us our instructions of what to do next. We believe our job is simply to live by the instructions and, of course, that's true. But the most fundamental of all instructions is to acknowledge and recognise that, without Christ, we can do nothing, he's actually involved in our day-to-day Christian living.

The Israelites forgot about this daily dependency on God as soon as they got to Kadesh-Barnea. They sent twelve spies into the land of Canaan, who were told to 'Find out what the people are like. Are they strong or weak? Are there many of them or are they few? Check the towns they live in, are they unwalled or are they fortified?' In other words 'Can we access them? Check the soil, is it fertile or poor? Bring back some samples.' And the spies went and did exactly that. They investigated the whole area and came back with pomegranates and grapes on their shoulders, so heavy it took two men to carry them on a pole. And when they got back, they said 'Moses, everything God said about the land is true. It's a land that flows with milk and honey. Look at the produce, look at the grapes and pomegranates. But there's a problem; there's a bunch of people there and they're powerful, some of them are giants. They're called the Amalekites and Jebusites, there's a bunch of them called Hittites and we don't like that name. There's another group called the Amorites. These folks are schooled in warfare.' And, of course, they were absolutely right the land of promise was going to be a land of warfare. Similarly for us, living in the fullness of God is not living detached from trouble; we're in warfare. The Israelites concluded 'We can't do it. We seem, like grasshoppers in our own eyes – and we looked the same to them.'

But, of the twelve spies, ten were bad and two were good. Joshua and Caleb, after hearing the report,

> tore their clothes and said to the entire Israelite assembly, 'The land we passed through and explored is exceedingly good. If the Lord is pleased with us, he will lead us into that land, a land flowing with milk and honey, and will give it to us. Only do not rebel against the Lord. And do not be afraid of the people of the land, because we will swallow them up. Their protection is gone, but the Lord is with us'
> (Num. 14:6-9).

So ten of the spies reported that, 'Yes, the land is great but we're never going to be able to conquer the people, they are far cleverer, we're just a group of nomads who've never held a weapon in our hands, we've just held tools in our hands, back in Egypt. These men are trained in warfare, we'll never do it.' But Joshua said, 'No,' and Caleb said, 'No.' 'It's absolutely true that they're far better than us in every human measurement but God is with us, this is God's business.' The Bible doesn't tell us how the people responded but they probably said, 'Don't be so spiritual, Joshua, you've got to be practical about these things, you've got to be realistic about them.' It's interesting that in Numbers 13 when God told Moses to send the spies in to explore Canaan, he said, 'This is the land I am giving to you.' 'Giving to you...' The Israelites didn't realise God's gift to them, they didn't understand what it meant to have God with them or to let him work on their behalf. They still didn't know what it meant to depend on him daily, they didn't have faith.

So most of the Israelites failed to enter Canaan and there are many Christians who fail to let God be God in their lives. Think for a moment. Are there things about your life that are inexplicable, apart from the fact that God is at work in you? You can't explain them except in terms of God. If we explain our lives and our circumstances in purely human terms, how different are we to the neighbours? One of the features of the Christian life is that our lives become explicable only in terms of God, working in us, working through us. Would your marriage be different if you weren't a Christian? If God would withdraw himself from you, this week, would you go home to a different marriage? Would your family life become different because you weren't living in the power of the risen Christ? Would your church even be different if God was withdrawn? I wonder.

- *Are there things about your life that are inexplicable, apart from the fact that God is at work in you?*
- *How can we cultivate a daily dependence on God and grow in our faith? What practical measures can we take so that increasingly we are letting God be God in our lives?*

FURTHER STUDY

Be encouraged by God's faithfulness. Using a concordance, look up some of the promises of God's faithfulness. In what particular areas does he promise to be faithful to us? Are there commitments we need to make to guarantee his faithfulness?

REFLECTION AND RESPONSE

Could you live without God for a day? Most of us would answer a vehement 'No' but realise that many times we go through a whole day without any consideration of him. Look back to the list you made in the 'Focus on the theme' section and your answers to the study questions – What do you put your faith in rather than God?

- Your health
- Your financial status
- Your spouse
- Your intelligence and education
- Your talents and gifts

All of these are good gifts from God but should not take the place of trusting him. On a piece of paper confess what/who you are trusting rather than God. On the other side of the paper write down a key relationship, situation or event you want to trust God in. Keep these pieces of paper in your Bible to remind you of the commitments and decisions you have made as a result of this study.

Conclude your time together by remembering why we can have complete faith in God – because of his faithfulness. Share verses of Scripture, prayers and songs focusing on God's utter faithfulness to his people.

CHAPTER 6

Rest

Aim: To grow in obedience and dependency on Christ's sufficiency

FOCUS ON THE THEME
Dream dreams together! On a piece of paper write down your idea of a perfect rest. It could be a weekend break at a spa hotel, two weeks lying on the beach in Spain or simply a quiet night in without the children. Fold up your paper and put all the sheets into a bowl. Go round the group each taking a piece of paper and trying to match the dream to the appropriate group member.

Read: Hebrews 3:7–4:13
Key verses: Hebrews 4:1-11

The reason why the writer to the Hebrews is retelling this whole Exodus story is not to discourage his readers, by saying, 'Look what they did and you are in danger of doing the same thing.' Having given them the bad news of their unbelief and their failure to live by faith and dependency on God, he says, 'Therefore, since the promise of entering his rest still stands, let us be careful that none of you be found to have fallen short of it' (4:1). The writer says 'this promise of entering God's rest still stands' and this word 'rest' occurs eleven times in these verses. What do we mean by rest? What does the Scripture mean by rest?

● *Despite having holidays and taking time off work our attempts to 'rest' are ultimately inadequate. Why?*

● *Why is Christ the only one who can give you perfect rest? What makes his rest something worth having?*

The writer defines it in verses 9-10 as a Sabbath-rest. He says in verse 9 'There remains, then, a Sabbath-rest for the people of God; for anyone who enters God's rest also rests from his own work'. In other words he is saying that there is a human experience that corresponds with the divine experience of God's rest, God's Sabbath-rest. Why did God rest at the end of creation on the seventh day? Did he rest because he was exhausted? God is inexhaustible, God didn't rest on the seventh day because he was tired. He rested because he was finished, big difference. The Sabbath rest is not a picture of exhaustion; it's a picture of sufficiency. That's why Adam's first day was a day of rest. He was created on the sixth day, it was a great day to be created and he might have said, 'What are we doing tomorrow?' And the reply came 'It's a day off.' Wonderful. Why did Adam have a day off on the first day of his life? Because he was demonstrating the principle of resting in God's sufficiency.

The Christian calendar only caught up with this principle after the resurrection of Jesus and the gift of the Holy Spirit and now we rest on the first day of the week, symbolically portraying that truth. God rested on the seventh day; man was to rest on the first day; we are to rest on the first day, in dependency on his sufficiency. And that's why the Christian life is called a life of rest, not a life of quietism. People sometimes talk about quietism, where you sit back and fold your arms and say, 'I just depend on God and I really don't discipline myself to do anything, just rely on God.' Ours is not a rest of passivism. It's a rest of Psalm 62 where the psalmist says, 'My soul find rest in

God alone ... He ... is my rock and my salvation; he is my fortress ... my refuge. Trust in him at all times'. What's he saying there? That you must learn to live in dependency on God.

● *What kind of rest are Christians getting on a Sunday, the first day of the week? Do you think this fulfils God's criteria?*

● *If rest is a daily dependence on God do we still need a specific day set aside to rest?*

Before the Israelites could 'rest' in Canaan they had to cross the river Jordan. Moses has died and Joshua is now leading the people. In Joshua 3 he says to them '...the Lord will do amazing things among you ... This is how you will know that the living God is among you...' But the Israelites just saw the obstacles before them and the barrier of the Jordan River. Joshua encouraged them, 'It's a new day, people of Israel ...the Lord will do amazing things'. Like them, our confidence and trust lies in the truth that 'The Lord will do amazing things.' Joshua went on 'This is how you will know God is among you, we'll obey what he says, put the Ark of the Covenant on our shoulders, the priests will carry it.' And as they placed their feet in the water, in obedient response and dependence on God, God parted the waves before them.

They came to the city of Jericho. God said, 'This is what I want you to do. Walk round the city, once a day, for six days. Put the priests in front, with the Ark of the Covenant and some trumpeters. And, when you get around the first time, blow your trumpet then come home. Go back and repeat this for six days. On the seventh day go round seven times, at the seventh time blow your trumpet and the walls will fall down.' Would these dramatic events happen because of some incredible trumpet playing? No. God delivers through our obedience; every act of God in the history of Israel is precipitated by an act of obedience. We don't sit back, arms folded, 'God, you do it, I'm watching. Save my neighbours please.' No, go and talk to your neighbours, in dependency on God. You act in obedience.

The Keswick Convention, which has been running now for a hundred and twenty-seven years, was formed on the basis of this issue of rest in the sufficiency and power of God. Canon Harford-Battersby, who was the vicar of St John's Church in Keswick, writes in his diary about being disillusioned with his own Christian life. 'I want to live a life of holiness,' he said 'and I can't.' American Robert Pearsall Smith was visiting this country, having meetings, and he arranged a big conference in Oxford. Harford-Battersby went from Keswick to Oxford to attend the conference. And a man called Evan Hopkins gave a message at that conference, in which he distinguished between seeking faith and resting faith. He took as his text the story of the nobleman whose son was healed in John 4.

> Hopkins explained that the nobleman had come to Christ with a *seeking faith*, begging Jesus to heal his son. When Jesus said, 'Thy son liveth', it was a statement of truth; he now had to believe as accomplished. This Hopkins described as *resting faith*, one of complete trust and dependence on God for everything he has promised, so much so that believers were invited to treat his promises as something already received ... This revelation to Harford-Battersby of the right to act in complete dependence on the full sufficiency of Christ, irrespective of the circumstances of one's life, was the catalyst that not only altered his outlook, but also transformed his experience.[1]

● *In what area of your life do you need resting faith? Which of God's promises do you need to trust him for?*

• *How would your behaviour and outlook alter if you treated that specific promise as already accomplished?*

He wrote in his diary of this time: 'Christ was revealed to me so powerfully and sweetly as the present Saviour in His all-sufficiency. I am His and do trust Him to make good all His promises to my soul.' Several years later, speaking at the last Keswick Convention before he died, he referred to that time. 'I got a revelation of Christ to my soul, so extraordinary, glorious and precious, that from that day to this it illuminated my life. I found He was all I wanted: I shall never forget it; the day and hour are present with me. How it humbled me and what peace it brought ... There are those who discovered a secret of power in service ... to which they were comparatively strangers, and their Christian life has flowed on ... with a sweet calm and inward peace which calls for continued thanksgiving.'[2]

He organised a four-day convention in Keswick in 1875 for the purpose of teaching other people the same thing.

Do you know the reality of Christ's sufficiency in your life? This is not just a passive dependency on God. In 4:11 the writer says; 'Let us, therefore, make every effort to enter that rest, so that no-one will fall by following their example of disobedience.' Doesn't that sound a little bit of a contradiction? 'Let us ... make every effort to enter that rest'? We don't say 'I need to make a big effort to go to bed'? What does he mean 'make every effort to enter into rest'? Some of you have a car parked outside. If I asked you 'What makes your car work?', you might say to me 'The engine.' And, of course, you'd be right. If you take the engine out of your car, all it would be good for would be keeping chickens in. You couldn't go anywhere. The engine is the power that takes the car down the road. Jesus Christ, by his indwelling Holy Spirit, is the power that enables us to live the Christian life. As he said 'Without me, you can do nothing.' An engine could say to a car, 'Without me, you can do nothing' and it would be true, the car couldn't go anywhere. But at the moment your car is outside with an engine under the bonnet doing nothing. Why? Because, in addition to the engine under the bonnet, you need to get in the seat, put your foot on the clutch, put it in gear, release the clutch, put your foot on the accelerator and steer it down the road. What's making the car go? Is it the engine? Is it the driver? What a silly question, it's both.

What makes the Christian life work? Is it Christ? Is it me? Silly question, it's both; we're workers together with God. Of course Christ, like the engine, is the indispensable ingredient, he works in us to will and to act according to his good pleasure. He works in us to motivate us, to direct us, to channel us. But you and I have to learn to become the driver, to exercise those disciplines that keep us in touch with God. The driver's job is to enable the power of the engine to make contact with the wheels and turn the thing down the road. So the responsibility of our walk with God is to enable his indwelling power to make contact with life as you bring him in to every situation and circumstance.

● *Brainstorm the disciplines that help you keep in touch with God, the practices that help train you to be obedient to him. Which have you found most helpful?*

But there are two big problems that Christians make. There are some Christians who think the Christian life is like learning the Highway Code. They've learnt it all, and they sit behind the wheel and make the right noises. They hold the wheel in the ten to two position because that's what the Highway Code says. They sit up straight, make the right noises, 'brmmmmm,' look out the window and say, 'I'm doing everything the Highway Code says but I'm not going anywhere.' They haven't learned that there's an engine under the bonnet. They haven't realised that all that God is, by his Holy Spirit, is available to us. But there are other folks who get excited about the engine. They sit behind the wheel, put their foot on the accelerator, right to the bottom, sit there, arms folded, 'rrrrrrrrwrrrrrrr wrrrrrrrwrrrrrrr.' The dust is blowing out down the street, every window in the street is rattling. 'Hallelujah, praise the Lord, isn't this wonderful?'

Then they look out the window. 'Why aren't I going anywhere?' Because it's not just the discipline of driving, nor is it the engine under the bonnet, it's both together. It's not just saying 'The Holy Spirit's taking charge of my life, that's it' or saying 'As long as I discipline myself the way I'm supposed to, it's going to work.' It's living in disciplined dependency on God that he might work through us.

That's why obedience to God and dependency on God cannot be separated. In fact obedience to God and dependency on God are like two wings on an aeroplane. Which wing do you think is the most important wing on an aeroplane? Obedience without dependency will lead to legalism. Dependency without obedience will lead to strange forms of mysticism. But obeying everything God tells us and depending on him for the resources will lead to dynamism.

● *Which are you more prone to do – be disciplined and accomplish tasks through your own willpower or passively invite the Holy Spirit to work on your behalf? What practical measures can you take to achieve the balance of obedience and dependency?*

'And there remains,' says the writer, 'a rest for the people of God.' He's writing this as a warning. If God is speaking you'd better make sure you hear, not so that you'll be equipped to pass a theological examination but so that it makes a difference to your heart. Then you can live in the richness of everything that's intended for you. God calls this 'entering into rest'. There'll be nothing that faces your life that is bigger than the resources you have in the Lord Jesus Christ. But you'll never prove it until you obey.

When Peter walked on the water of the lake of Galilee, it was Christ who enabled him to break the natural laws of nature. When he began to fall and drown, Jesus said, 'Oh you of little faith, you stopped trusting me.' Although Peter enjoyed the power of God, enabling him to walk on the water, if you're going to walk on the water what have you got do? You've got to get out of the boat. That means you've got to say, 'Lord, I'm going to step out in obedience to you and take risks of obedience that will get me into Canaan.' There's a battle on every page of the book of Joshua but the wonderful thing is there's also victory because it's God who will give us the land.

- *As an encouragement to one another, share examples of when you have 'stepped out of the boat', when you've 'entered into rest' in obedience and dependence on God. What did you learn, how did your faith grow?*

FURTHER STUDY

This section on rest in Hebrews 4 concludes with verses 12-13, that deal with the power of the word of God and God's all-seeing eyes. Can you explain how these themes relate to the preceding eleven verses?

REFLECTION AND RESPONSE

In Psalm 62 David talks about his soul finding rest in God. Like David, when we're resting in God we take time to listen to him. Psalm 62:11-12 says, 'One thing God has spoken, two things have I heard: that you, O God, are strong, and that you, O Lord, are loving.'

Spend time resting in God's presence. Don't be afraid of the silence; perhaps have some music gently playing in the background. Sit comfortably and allow God to speak to you. Make time to practice this discipline of stillness during the week. Rest in his presence as a way of showing your dependence on him and your obedience to his will, rather than being driven by your 'to do' list.

REVIEW OF HEBREWS 3:7–4:13

This section of Hebrews is based on the Exodus account. Take time to reflect on your own exodus experience. Consider:

• Egypt – the slavery to sin you have been released from

• The Passover lamb – Jesus' sacrifice on your behalf

• Manna – Jesus' feeding you on your spiritual journey

• Canaan – the rest that God has planned for you

If it is appropriate, share communion together, remembering that our exodus is only possible because of Christ's exodus. As you take the elements, reflect on God's great faithfulness. And, with that in mind, don't be afraid to press on to whatever Jordan or Jericho God has in store for you. Learn the lessons of Hebrews – don't have a hard heart but live a life of faith, fulfilling God's purpose for you and enjoying all that he has planned for you.

POINTS TO PONDER

• What have you learnt about God?

• What have you learnt about yourself?

• What actions or attitudes do you need to change as a result?

---

[1] Charles Price and Ian Randall, *Transforming Keswick* (OM Publishing: Carlisle, 2000)

[2] Charles Price and Ian Randall, *Transforming Keswick* (OM Publishing: Carlisle, 2000)

CHAPTER 7

Jesus our priest

Aim: To affirm our confidence in Jesus' role as priest

FOCUS ON THE THEME
Divide the group into two. One half of the group should come up with a list of Christian jargon words or words found in the Bible that you wouldn't use in common speech. Take turns describing these words to the other group. The others have to try and guess the word that is being described as quickly as possible. You'll probably find there are some words you have difficulty describing and others like 'priest' and 'covenant' that are not used much today but have a rich meaning and help us understand the story of the Bible.

Read: Hebrews 4:14–10:39
Key verses: Hebrews 6:19–7:28

The next section of Hebrews, from 4:14–10:39, speaks primarily about the priesthood of Christ and the new covenant of which he is the priest. There is an interlude in chapter six where he warns against apostasy and falling away but we will look at that in a subsequent chapter.

The word 'priest' is not a strong word in Protestant vocabulary, particularly in non-conformist circles. It's a word that never once appears in the thirteen letters of Paul, it doesn't appear in the letters of Peter, it doesn't appear in the letter of James, it doesn't appear in the writings of John, and it doesn't appear in the epistle of Jude. This is the only

Epistle in which the word priest occurs and it occurs twenty-eight times, in every chapter from chapter 2 to 10, and then as the writer sums up in the end of chapter 13, it's mentioned again. Twenty-four of those 28 references have to do with the priesthood of Christ. The writer's main theme is that Christ is a priest forever of a new covenant. And of course, the Hebrews knew all about the priesthood because right at the very core of their worship was the function of the priests. If the priests didn't turn up, everything closed down.

● *Brainstorm everything you know about the role of the priest in Israelite society. What tasks did Eli, Samuel, Aaron, John the Baptist's father Zechariah, Annas and Caiaphas perform on behalf of the people?*

Let me define these words 'priesthood' and 'covenant' so that we know exactly what we're talking about. A priest is an intermediary who stands between two parties and connects them with each other. As Hebrews 5:1 explains, 'Every high priest is selected from among men and is appointed to represent them in matters related to God, to offer gifts and sacrifices for sins.' The priest stood between God and humanity for the purpose of bringing them together and reconnecting them.

The second significant term in these verses is the word 'covenant'. A covenant is an agreement made between two parties, not necessarily equal parties but agreed to by both parties. God made several covenants with Israel throughout their history. Prior to that he made a covenant with Noah who predated Abraham and therefore was not a Jew. He made a covenant with Abraham in Genesis 17. That covenant had to do with a group of people – Abraham's offspring; a certain place – the land of Canaan; and a particular purpose – that by blessing them he would bless the whole world. And basically, the story of the Old

Testament is the story of keeping these three peas in the same pod. If you like, the story of the Old Testament is keeping the right people in the right place for the right purpose. You get the right people in the wrong place, they won't fulfil the purpose; get the wrong people in the right place, they won't fulfil the purpose; get the right people in the right place, who forget the purpose and they're in trouble. The Israelites were taken off into Babylonian exile to teach them, 'You've forgotten the whole purpose.' But get the right people in the right place, fulfilling the right purpose and you're on track.

In chapter 8 the author of Hebrews is referring to the covenant God made with Moses on Mount Sinai. The agreement was that the people would obey the law God had given (see Ex. 24:7). Now the writer describes this covenant as obsolete (8:13). Why? Because the people were unable to fulfil their side of the covenant. That was no surprise to God; he knew that, long before he made the covenant with them. And so he replaced the obsolete covenant with a new one. Jesus is the priest of the new covenant; as Hebrews 9:15 says, 'Christ is the mediator of a new covenant'. The priesthood of the new covenant may seem a distant concept to our lives and it may seem irrelevant but keep reading. Your confidence in the covenant will be dependent on your confidence in the priest of the new covenant. He is the one who acts as the mediator between us and God.

- *What other people or methods do we use to try and gain access to God, what other mediators do we rely on? For example, do we expect our pastor's prayers to influence God more than our prayers?*

- *What do we learn about God from the fact that he replaced the old covenant with a new one and he replaced the old priesthood with a perfect priest?*

Let's look at this priest of the new covenant. Remember this letter is written to Hebrews, Jewish people, who would be able to understand the concept of Jesus' priesthood because they were familiar with the priesthood of Israel. The people were familiar with the Levitical priesthood or what the book of Hebrews calls the Aaronic priesthood. This was the succession of priests that began with Aaron, Moses' brother. Aaron was the first priest in Israel and when he died his son, Eleazar, replaced him as priest. And, shortly afterwards, before the Israelites entered Canaan, the Lord set apart the whole tribe of Levi, of which Moses and Aaron were members, to serve as priests (Deut. 10).

However, when the writer of Hebrews reflects on the Levitical or Aaronic priesthood, there are some big problems with its suitability as a type or picture of Christ. First of all, Jesus was not a Levite, he was from the tribe of Judah and the Levitical priesthood was a hereditary priesthood. And so, being from the tribe of Judah he was automatically disqualified from being a priest (7:14). To add to this, the Levitical priesthood was not a very good model for the Lord Jesus. For example, the priests were subject to weaknesses (5:2); they always had to deal with their own sins before addressing the sins of the people (7:27); they could not clear the conscience of the worshipper (9:9); they had to repeat the same sacrifice again and again, their work was never finished (10:11). And therefore the writer says the priesthood of Aaron does not accurately or adequately foreshadow the priesthood of Christ. So he rummages around in the little bit of Old Testament history that's left once you take out the Aaronic priesthood and he finds an obscure man who appears once, in two verses, back in the book of Genesis, and then he disappears again. His name was Melchizedek. And the writer concludes that Jesus, the priest of this new covenant, will be of the order of Melchizedek (5:8-10).

Now Melchizedek is one of the most mysterious characters in the Bible. He appears first in Genesis 14:18-20. Abraham has just come back from defeating a coalition of kings and it says 'Then Melchizedek king of Salem brought out bread and wine. He was priest of God Most High, and he blessed Abram, saying, "Blessed be Abram by God Most High, Creator of heaven and earth. And blessed be God Most High, who delivered your enemies into your hand." Then Abram gave him a tenth of everything.' Then he disappears but a thousand years later jumps up in Psalm 110, a messianic Psalm. It is from Psalm 110:4, 'The Lord has sworn and will not change his mind: "You are a priest for ever, in the order of Melchizedek"' that the author of Hebrews drew his inspiration. So a thousand years later in the book of Hebrews Melchizedek is mentioned eight times in chapters 5 and 7. He's a once a millennium man.

There are five things the writer identifies about Melchizedek which make him representative of Christ (7:1-3). The first thing is that Melchizedek has no genealogy. Let me explain the significance of this. The priesthood of Israel was based entirely on genealogy; it was the hereditary principle that enabled a person to become a priest. You had to be of the tribe of Levi and trace your ancestry back to Aaron. By Jewish law a man could not become a priest unless he could trace his pedigree. After the exile, when the Persians allowed the Israelites back to Judah, Ezra explains that many returning Levites 'searched for their family records, but they could not find them and so were excluded from the priesthood as unclean' (Ezra 2:62). If you couldn't trace your genealogy nothing could make you a priest: character had nothing to do with it, ability had nothing to do with it, gift had nothing to do with it: it was purely hereditary.

In contrast Melchizedek was 'Without father or mother, without genealogy, without beginning of days or end of life, like the Son he remains a priest for ever' (7:3). Now what does this mean, that Melchizedek had no genealogy? Some have suggested that Melchizedek was a Christophany or a theophany. That is a physical incarnation of God, a pre-incarnate appearance of Christ, such as the angel of the Lord who appeared to Moses in the burning bush. I don't think he was. A common rabbinical way of interpreting Scripture was to argue as much from silence as from substance. In other words, where the Scriptures say nothing, assume nothing. So the writer's not suggesting that Melchizedek was some freak of nature with no father or mother, or that he might be an angel; but rather, that the silence about his family background and the context from which Melchizedek came are as inspired by God as the details we do have about his life. The writer is saying that from the silence of Scripture we will treat Melchizedek as though he was a man with no father, no mother, and no genealogy. The Hebrew readers would have been familiar with this school of interpretation and it would have struck them that to introduce a priest without genealogy is to reverse all the rules of hereditary priesthood. Melchizedek is a type, a picture, of Jesus. Just as Melchizedek had no father, mother or genealogy, neither did Jesus in his ultimate origin. He was born of Mary in Bethlehem in his human incarnation, but he was pre-existent to his humanity. As John 1:1-2 says, 'In the beginning was the Word, and the Word was with God, and the Word was God. He was with God in the beginning'. Whenever the beginning began, he was already there and in that sense, like Melchizedek, he has no father or mother.

● *Why is it significant that despite his human origin in Bethlehem, it is valid to say Jesus had neither father nor mother?*

● *If Jesus had no father why do we use the terms 'God the Father' and 'God the Son'? What kind of concepts do these terms help us understand?*

Secondly, Melchizedek is a representative of Jesus because as verse 3 says, Melchizedek lasts for ever, 'like the Son of God he remains a priest for ever.' Again this is arguing from the silence of Scripture that mentions nothing of Melchizedek's death.

● *Look at Hebrews 7:23-25. What does Jesus' eternal priesthood mean for us?*

Thirdly, Melchizedek's name means 'king of righteousness ... king of peace', verse 2. These themes of righteousness and kingship correspond to Christ, as the writer explains in Hebrews 1:8 when he writes 'But about the Son he says, "Your throne, O God, will last for ever and ever, and righteousness will be the sceptre of your kingdom."'

Fourthly, when Abraham returned from a victorious battle he gave Melchizedek a tithe, ten per cent of everything he possessed (v4). Now the Levitical priest collected a tenth from the people, it was their legal duty and obligation. But Abraham had no obligation to pay a tithe to Melchizedek; he gave it voluntarily. And the point is that Melchizedek is a picture of Jesus our priest and our response to him, my response to him, is not one of compulsion. Our response is voluntary, 'whosoever will may come.' Of course, the Holy Spirit is involved in our coming to Christ but we're not forced to come, the way is open to us.

● *We are not under compulsion to respond to Christ but to what extent is it true we have a debt and obligation towards him?*

The final correlation between Jesus and Melchizedek appears in 7:26-28. The writer says 'Such a high priest meets our need – one who is holy, blameless, pure, set apart from sinners, exalted above the heavens. Unlike the other high priests, he does not need to offer sacrifices day after day, first for his own sins, and then for the sins of the people. He sacrificed for their sins once for all when he offered himself.' He makes the connection between Melchizedek and Christ, who offered sin once for all. The day Jesus Christ cried out from the cross, 'It is finished' there was no need for any more blood to be shed. On that day the Temple curtain was torn from top to the bottom. That was the barrier that had separated the Holy of Holies from the people and which could only be approached by a priest with blood, on the Day of Atonement. That curtain was torn, not as a human act from bottom to top, but as a divine act from top to bottom, and from that moment every priest in Israel was out of a job. There was no need for any more priests because Jesus offered himself once and for all. And as 8:1 says, he 'sat down at the right hand of the throne of the Majesty in heaven'. The Levitical priest never sat down.

● *Why was being 'holy, blameless, pure, set apart from sinners, exalted about the heavens' essential for Jesus to be the perfect priest?*

Having explained all of this, the writer to the Hebrews concludes this qualifies Jesus as our priest and our mediator. So the grounds of our access to God and our accessibility to God is not based on our personal credentials, any more than it was based on the personal credentials of the Israelites. They could only approach God because of the credentials of the priest. And we have a priest who is totally adequate: who you are, what your history is, what your background is, what sins you're up to your neck in, are irrelevant. You can approach God through this priest; because it's the priest that is acceptable to God, it's the priest who addresses God and reconciles us. And that's why he says in chapter 4:14,16, 'Therefore, since we have a great high priest who has gone through the heavens, Jesus the Son of God, let us hold firmly to the faith we profess ... Let us then approach the throne of grace with confidence' (Confidence in what? Confidence in the priest who has access to the Father) 'so that we may receive mercy and find grace to help us in our time of need.'

- *What does it mean to you to know that your access to God is not dependent on your credentials but based on Jesus' credentials?*

- *'How would you respond to the following comments:*
  - *'I couldn't possibly become a Christian; I have done too many things wrong.'*
  - *'Ultimately we have all sinned against God so he is the only one able to grant forgiveness to people. It is not my job to forgive anyone.'*
  - *'I know Jesus gives me direct access to God but I still find it helpful to discuss my problems and needs with other people, particularly church leaders and mature Christians'.*

FURTHER STUDY
Jesus is not only our priest: what other roles does he have? Which of his tasks are completed and which ones is he still performing? What criteria make him supreme in all of these roles?

REFLECTION AND RESPONSE
Our priest didn't wear robes, he hung naked on a cross, with nails in his hands and a crown of thorns on his head. He didn't have the trappings of a priest or even the traditional qualifications and yet he

is our perfect priest because he has access to God. Consider Jesus: because he is our perfect priest

- Hold firmly to the faith you profess (Heb. 4:14)
- Receive mercy and grace in your time of need (Heb. 4:16)
- Draw near to God (Heb. 7:19)
- Be assured of your salvation (Heb. 7:25)
- Serve God without guilt (Heb. 9:14)
- Know your eternal inheritance is secure (Heb. 9:15)
- Accept you have been made holy (Heb. 10:10)

Spend time in quiet talking to your priest – confess your sins, ask for his help and strength, bring before him whatever needs you have.

As a group, ask Jesus to intercede on your behalf for broader issues. Bring to him your church needs, any concerns in your community, and prayer requests for the nation.

CHAPTER 8

The new covenant

Aim: Learning to live in the power of the new covenant

FOCUS ON THE THEME
- What are you like at making and keeping promises?
- What's the hardest promise you've ever made?
- What's the strangest promise you've ever made?
- What was the first promise you broke?

The new covenant is God's promise to us and our promise to him but it's a promise we can keep because he gives us his strength.

Read: Hebrews 4:14–10:39
Key verses: Hebrews 8:7-12

Now let's look at this new covenant that the priest Christ Jesus is introducing us to. Hebrews 8:7-12 is a direct quotation from Jeremiah 31 when God had spoken about the covenant he would bring to the house of Israel. Clearly there was something wrong with the first covenant or it wouldn't have been replaced (v7). So what was wrong with it?

We mentioned earlier that a covenant is an agreement between two parties; both need to agree to it. Moses came down the mountain and said to the people 'This is the law of God, what are you going to do about it?' The people replied 'We will keep the law.' They repeated this declaration in the book of Deuteronomy, they said it again in the book of Joshua and at various other intervals. But God found fault with the people (8:8). There was nothing wrong with the law, only something wrong with the people, their inability to keep it. So now he says, 'I am going to bring a new covenant.' But, interestingly, the new covenant is about the same law. But God said this time 'I'll put my laws in their minds.' It used to be on tablets of stone; now 'I will … write them on their hearts' (8:10).

- *If the people were unable to keep the old covenant, what value did it have?*

The fundamental difference between the two covenants was that in the old covenant, the onus was on the people. The old covenant was based on the people remembering the Ten Commandments. 'You shall have no other gods before me,' 'You shall not make for yourself an idol,' 'You shall not misuse the name of the Lord your God.' You, you, you... And, in their naïveté, they said, 'Sure, we'll do it.' In contrast, in the new covenant, the onus is on God. God said 'This is the covenant I will make with the house of Israel … I will put my laws in their minds and write them on their hearts. I will be their God … I will forgive their wickedness and will remember their sins no more.' (vv 10-12) This is a significant difference. The first covenant was 'You do it'; in the new covenant God said 'I will do it.'

- *Brainstorm all the other types of covenants you are familiar with. How does this new covenant compare in terms of the power and responsibilities of the two parties and the benefits they would receive from the covenant?*

Let's look at this new covenant. Firstly it's about a *new righteousness*. God said in verse 10 'I will put my laws in their minds and write them on their hearts.' The new covenant was still going to involve the law but it was going to be internal in its operation. You see, the law doesn't change; it could not change, because the law is a revelation of the character of God and God's character does not change. The reason why God said, in the law, 'You shall not steal' is because God doesn't steal, it's an expression of his character. When it says, 'You shall not commit adultery,' it's because God is totally faithful and it's an expression of his character. So the law doesn't change, that's why Jesus said, in the Sermon on the Mount, 'not one dot, not one cross of a T will disappear from the law.' God doesn't change, doesn't wind down, doesn't grow up, doesn't get better, and doesn't get worse. So the law, which expresses his character, doesn't change; it's still the same law but instead of being written on the tablets of stone, it was to be written in their hearts and minds.

Now the law has a very interesting history in Scripture. When God gave it to Moses on Mount Sinai, it was the only part of the biblical text written by the finger of God himself. Men, moved by the Holy Spirit, wrote the rest but this is the only part of Scripture that God himself wrote. So the law came down from Mount Sinai with the highest pedigree possible. The historical books of the Old Testament record the law as the plumbline for measuring human behaviour. The poetic books of the Old Testament meditate on the law. The prophetic books of the Old Testament preach the law. When you get to the end of the Old Testament, the law still has an esteemed position. When Jesus came on the scene he affirmed the law (Mt. 5). The law remains fully intact until you get into the epistles of Paul, in particular, when suddenly it becomes a dirty word. Galatians 3:10 says 'All who rely on observing the law are under a curse'. Chapter 3 goes on to say 'Christ redeemed us from the curse of the law' (v13). Suddenly the law that came from God himself and had been highly regarded for generations is our jailer, it's our oppressor.

This change in perspective was not a problem with the law itself, because the law reveals the character of God. The problem was that the law was given to Moses on tablets of stone and it was external. It could demand righteousness, it could demand what was right, but it could never accomplish it. All the law could do was house train people. You house train animals, you teach them to behave on the basis of consequences. We have a couple of cats in our home. We got them as kittens and had to house train them. We've taught them to eat outside the back door; they know they are not allowed to eat anything in the house. They know that there are certain places they are not allowed to sleep, so they don't. You never see our cats jumping onto the counter in the kitchen and eating any food that's lying around. If you came to our house you'd be impressed because we have taught them to behave perfectly and they do, as long as we're there.

But if we leave the house in a hurry and leave a bit of food out on the counter, you can be sure, when we get back there will be tongue prints in the butter. Because when we leave the house, one will open one eye, the other will open the other eye, they'll look across and say, 'They've gone and when they've gone, we couldn't care less how we behave. We're only concerned that when they're here there are consequences if we eat the butter.' All the law can ever do is house train you. There are a lot of evangelical Christians who have been house trained and that's about it. How do you know when you've been house trained? It's how you live when nobody's looking. If you live one way when nobody's looking and a different way when people are looking, you've not been sanctified; you've just been house trained. That's why legalism is not only unhelpful, it is anti-Christian. We can teach people to behave legally, just keep the law but the problem with the law is it's the opposite of faith. It's the enemy of truth in the sense that it's the jailer that imprisons us.

- *Regarding this issue of being house trained or sanctified, how would you respond to an associate minister who said, 'I have a certain role to perform. It's not that I am putting on a persona, it's just that people have certain expectations of me. Isn't it true that we all put on a some sort of brave face to the world?'*
- *How can we make it more and more true that the Christian image we present to people on a Sunday is matched by how we act when nobody's looking?*

Now the new covenant does not impose a law from the outside, it places the law of God inside. The end product is the same but the law is now written on our hearts and put in our minds. In his vision of the new covenant, Ezekiel says, 'I will put my Spirit in you' (Ezek. 36:27). As Jesus explained to the disciples in the upper room, the Holy Spirit 'lives with you and will be in you' (Jn. 14:17). That's why the disciples were different men after Pentecost. The Spirit of God was in them, the law was written in their hearts and minds. And for us too, it's not simply about what we do in response to 'You shall not, you shall not.' It's now a response to what God does, when he says, 'I will move you to follow my decrees and keep my laws.' You see, not only is there a new priest operating for us now, our righteousness depends on this priest; but there is also a new power operating in us; the indwelling presence of the Spirit of Jesus Christ. It's the same law but based on different locations. The new covenant doesn't revise the law; it simply relocates the law. It's no longer on tablets of stone kept in the Ark of the covenant in the Holy of Holies in the Temple in Jerusalem. It's the same law but it's placed in your heart.

● *We have got the Spirit of Jesus Christ inside of us. How can we learn to listen to what the Spirit of Jesus is telling us?*

Because the indwelling presence of the Holy Spirit enables us to implement this new covenant, what were commands under the old covenant actually become promises under the new covenant. Let me illustrate this for you. I heard a story of a man who was converted to Christ in a prison. He was in for stealing but when he was released, he wanted to visit a church. He'd never been to a church in his life before so he just picked one at random on the first Sunday of his release. He went in, sat down, looked up to the front of the church and there, on the wall, was written the Ten Commandments. He thought to himself 'that's the last thing I want to see. I know my history, I know my background, I know my failure, and I know my weakness. The last thing I want to see are those laws that condemn me.' I don't know whether the service was a bit long or a bit tedious but he began to read the commandments again. And as he did so he discovered he was reading them totally differently to any way he'd read them before. Previously, when he'd read them, they'd said things like, 'You shall not steal,' it was a command. But, this morning, when he read it, it said 'You shall not steal,' it was a promise. If I'm going to put words in his mouth he might have said, 'Thank you, Lord.' Why? 'Because I put my law in your mind, I'm your God, that's why.' It used to say 'You shall not commit adultery,' it was a command, but this morning it said 'You shall not commit adultery,' it was a promise. 'Thank you, Lord,' he might have said. Why? 'Because I put my law in your mind, in your heart.' Everything that had been commands, previously, suddenly, he discovered, were promises.

This truth is explained in Romans 8:3-4: 'For what the law could not do because it was weakened by the sinful flesh, God did by the sending of his Son to be a sin offering and so he condemns sin in sinful man in order that the righteous requirements of the law might be fully met in us, who walk on after the Spirit; not after the flesh but after the Spirit.' What the law couldn't do, God did. Why? By giving his Son first as our substitute, as a sin offering and then by his indwelling Holy Spirit that the righteous requirements of the law might be fully met. When the law says 'You shall not steal,' you don't. Why? Because you're more disciplined than you used to be? No, the Spirit of God is in you, he places that hunger and thirst for righteousness, he works in you to will and to do according to God's pleasure. And it works, not from the outside in as the law had done, but from the inside out as the Spirit does. That's why righteousness in the New Testament is fruit. Philippians 1:11 speaks of being filled with the fruit of righteousness. Fruit is a consequence of life, it flows out naturally because the Spirit of God is in us. And the discipline we need to exercise is not a discipline to get godliness into our lives; it's a discipline that allows God to get out of our lives.

So if you have a problem with stealing, there's a promise for you in Exodus 20. It used to be written on tablets of stone but now it's written, by the Spirit, in your heart: it says 'You shall not steal.' Thank him for that. You may be facing sexual temptation you can hardly cope with. There's a promise in Exodus 20 written by the Spirit in your heart that says 'You shall not commit adultery.' Isn't that good to know? Nobody living in the fullness of the Spirit commits adultery. If you struggle with greed, there's a promise in Exodus 20 'You shall not covet.' Some of us get our priorities all mixed up and out of balance. Here's a promise; it used to be a command written on tablets of stone, now it's a promise written by the Spirit in your heart, 'You shall have no other gods before me.' You'll get your priorities right, when God is God. So this new righteousness doesn't just work from the outside in, forcing us to keep trying to keep the law and do better. It's a righteousness that is a release from the inside out as the Spirit of God writes the law of God in our hearts.

● *Explain, in terms of the Spirit of God and the new covenant, what happens when we do sin; when we covet or steal, for example.*

● *How do we get back into a right relationship with God after we have sinned? What steps should we take ourselves to avoid a repeat performance?*

The new covenant also means a *new relationship*. It's actually the new relationship that leads to the new righteousness. God says 'I will be their God, and they will be my people ... No longer will a man teach his neighbour, or a man his brother, saying "Know the Lord," because they will all know me, from the least of them to the greatest' (8:10-11). How is this law in our hearts possible? It comes from knowing God; it's in knowing God that everything else has its source. 2 Peter 1:3 says 'His divine power has given us everything we need for life and godliness through our knowledge of him who called us by his own glory and goodness.' 2 Peter 3:18 says 'grow in the grace and knowledge of our Lord and Saviour Jesus Christ.' That's why you spend time reading your Bible, not to get to know the Bible but to get to know Christ, who's revealed through the Scriptures. The living word is revealed through the written Word.

The least of us to the greatest will know God. That's an interesting progression. Knowledge of God is not obtained: it is received, it's dependent on revelation. As Jesus said in Matthew 11:25, 'I praise you, Father, Lord of heaven and earth, because you have hidden these things from the wise and the learned, and revealed them to little children. Yes, Father, for this was your good pleasure.' And that's why we come, in humility as children, and say, 'Lord, reveal more of yourself.' And out of this new relationship – knowing God, knowing whom we have believed, not knowing what we have believed – comes a new righteousness. The more you know Christ, the more you become like him. It's a process; we're being transformed from one degree of glory to another, in his image. The more you know him, the more you become like him.

● *Who have you known that was really like Christ? What was it about them that you admired? What lessons can you learn from them about how to become Christ-like?*

This amazing new relationship is possible because it's based on a *new redemption.* 'I ... will remember their sins no more' (v12). We already mentioned that the sacrifices offered could never cleanse the conscience of the worshipper in Israel. Hebrews 10:1 speaks of this ritual happening 'endlessly year after year'. Hebrews 10:11 says 'Day after day every priest stands and performs his religious duties; again and again he offers the same sacrifices, which can never take away sins.' Notice the routine, the dullnesses, 'again and again, day after day ... never, never, never, never.' But now, he says, 'your sins are remembered no more.'

It's not that the blood of bulls and goats had no meaning, of course it did, but it acted a bit like a cheque. A cheque is a meaningless, worthless piece of paper. The worth of a cheque depends on the account on which it's drawn. The first cheque I ever received was for one million pounds. It was from my school friend, written on his father's chequebook. I never cashed it because I knew his father! The paper is worthless, it's only valid for as much as there is cash in the bank. What if you've no cash in the bank? Well, you can postdate a cheque. You want to buy something and you haven't got the money, you can arrange, with the person from whom you're buying, to postdate your cheque to the end of the month, when you get your salary. You write the cheque and the debt is covered but it's not removed. Now the blood of bulls and goats were like cheques; worthless in themselves, they covered sin but did not remove it. And when Jesus, on the cross, cried 'It is finished', do you know what he was saying? There's cash in the bank and every Old Testament believer cashed their cheque. Now, we're dealing with the real currency, not the postdated cheque. The real currency is not the blood of bulls and goats but the precious blood of Christ. This is the cash, the real currency that addresses the Father and doesn't just cover sin; it removes sin to the extent 'I will remember your sins no more.'

One of the biggest needs that many Christians have is really, really to believe that God remembers our sins no more. Because we confess the same sins again and again thinking, 'I wonder if I'm really cleared.' I talked to someone the other day who told me that for thirty-eight years she had confessed the same sin almost every day. She had no assurance she was forgiven and was scared of judgement day because this sin might still be there. Do you know the marvellous thing is that although we don't deserve it, 'I will remember it no more.' That doesn't mean God is forgetful, it means he never recalls it, never brings it up again. I really wish we believed that, it would liberate some of us.

When God said he would remember our sins no more this has nothing to do with our sins, our iniquities, nothing to do with what we deserve, but everything to do with the quality of our priest. This priest didn't just offer sacrifices, he was the sacrifice and it's by the blood of Jesus we, with confidence, have access to God. The whole saving work of Christ is encompassed in this new covenant. Our sins are forgiven at the cross. Having been forgiven, we come to the empty tomb that we might get to know the living Christ and the power of his resurrection. And from there we go to Pentecost where God says 'I'll put my Spirit in you and I'll move you to follow my decrees and keep my law.' This is the new covenant. Are you living in the good of it? Are you glad you're a Christian?

● *What difference would it make to you and to how you treat others if you really believed God remembers our sin no more? Would you treat yourself differently?*

FURTHER STUDY

Look at the various covenants in the Old Testament. Throughout history, how have God's promises stayed the same, and how have they changed? What do the covenants teach us about God's priorities for us?

REFLECTION AND RESPONSE

In silence, for the last time, recall the sin that has bound you with guilt. If it helps, write it down on a piece of paper and then shred the paper as a symbol that just as God will not recall your sin any more, neither will you. Make a commitment today to live in the power of the new covenant.

As a group, praise God for everything he has done to be in a relationship with us. This supreme God does not stay at a distance but wants to be 'our God'. Who else has loved you, who else has made such a commitment to you as our God?

REVIEW OF HEBREWS 4:14-10:39

Reread Hebrews 4:14-10:39. Notice that the culmination of these verses concerning our perfect priest and the new and lasting covenant is: 'Therefore, brothers, since we have confidence to enter the Most Holy Place by the blood of Jesus ...

- 'Let us draw near to God' (10:22)
- 'Let us hold unswervingly to the hope we profess' (10:23)
- 'Let us consider how we may spur one another on towards love and good deeds' (10:24)
- 'Let us not give up meeting together ... but let us encourage one another daily' (10:25)

Measuring yourself against these criteria, how well are you living by the new covenant?

Take time to renew your focus – Jesus' priesthood, the new covenant and our living in the good of it is all because 'He who is coming will come and will not delay' (10:37). What do you want your priorities, values and behaviour to be when Jesus returns? What changes do you need to make now, what practices do you need to give time to now?

POINTS TO PONDER

- What have you learnt about God?
- What have you learnt about yourself?
- What actions or attitudes do you need to change as a result?

CHAPTER 9

Faith sees beyond circumstances

Aim: Learning to trust God patiently in difficult times

> **FOCUS ON THE THEME**
> When hard times hit, what is your instinctive reaction?
> • Phone your mother/best friend
> • Ask God 'Why?'
> • Pray
> • Worry
> • Keep a low profile until the crisis passes
> • See them as opportunities to develop your character
>
> Changing how we instinctively respond to difficulties, and training ourselves to respond with a faith that trusts God despite the circumstances, takes a lifetime of practice as Abraham and Moses found out.

Read: Hebrews 11:1- 40
Key verses: Hebrews 11:8-19, 23-29

Hebrews 11 is probably the best-known chapter in this book. It's the gallery of men and women of faith. But it's not just a series of success stories. It is full of apparent failures, stories of conflict, difficulties, and of tragedy, from a human perspective. And yet, in all these circumstances, God is doing something. There are fifteen characters in this chapter; though, of the forty verses, nineteen of them are devoted to two men in particular; Abraham and Moses.

The chapter begins with that great statement, in verse 1, 'Faith is being sure of what we hope for'. But the section really starts in 10:33 when the writer recalls 'Sometimes you were publicly exposed to insult and persecution; at other times you stood side by side with those who were so treated. You sympathised with those in prison and joyfully accepted the confiscation of your property ...' Why? '... because you knew that you yourselves had better and lasting possessions' (10:33-34). So this idea of faith as being sure of what we hope for, means that faith functions in the understanding that there is better to come outside of this life. There is a lot to enjoy from God in this life, of course. But when, in the purposes of God, life is tough, situations are hard and persecution is real, faith is being sure that the best is yet to come.

Verse 6 is a key verse; 'Without faith it is impossible to please God, because anyone who comes to him must believe that he exists and that he rewards those who earnestly seek him.' If faith is dependence on God, simply trusting and depending on him, what pleases God primarily is the measure of our dependency on him. Romans 14:23 makes the general statement 'everything that does not come from faith is sin.' This means that what does not derive from dependence on God, by definition, derives from independence of God. So whatever does not derive from faith is sin. Living in sin is not only running off with your neighbour's wife or taking home the Sunday morning offering plate and putting it under your mattress. Living in sin is living independently of God. I can preach a sermon to you in sin, if I'm doing so independently of God instead of in dependence on him.

● *How can we measure our independence/dependence on God?*

It's a shame that living by faith has become, in evangelical circles, a technical term for what missionaries do who don't get paid. We say they 'live by faith'. Somebody once asked me if I lived by faith and I said 'Yes, do you?' And he replied 'No, I've got a job.' I didn't like the implication of that, so I said 'So have I actually, why do you suddenly talk about your job?' He explained, 'What I meant was, do you get paid for what you do?' And I said, 'That has nothing to do, biblically, about whether I live by faith or not. Living by faith has nothing to do with my finances; living by faith has everything to do with my dependency on God.' And whether you're earning a hundred thousand pounds a year or you stepped out in a obedience to God with no guarantee of an income is actually irrelevant to whether you live by faith. We're going to see that these men and women in chapter 11 were people who discovered that, even when it comes to having babies, it's by faith. Every part of life operates on the basis of faith.

● *Share examples of ways you are dependent on God:*
  – *In your workplace*
  – *In your family life*
  – *In your marriage*
  – *In your church ministry*

Faith sees beyond circumstances. What I mean is there are many, many events that come into our lives and if somebody were to say 'Where is God in this situation? Where are the fingerprints of God in this event?'; you would have to shrug your shoulders and say, 'I don't know.' Paul sets up the contrast in 2 Corinthians 5:7, 'We live by faith, not by sight.' In other words, what you can see and living by faith are not always the same thing. Sometimes you live in dependency on God in the dark, you cannot see what he is doing. If you need an example, look at Abraham's life.

● *How does walking by faith, not sight, work out in practice?*
  What advice would you give the following people?
  - *'I have had a job offer. It seems like something I'd really*
    like to do but it would mean moving away from home. I'm
    ready for a new challenge and I feel a peace about accepting
    it but I just wish God would make his will clear to me.'
  - *'I've had offers at three different universities. How do I*
    know which one God wants me to go to?'
  - *'I really felt God gave me this job as a manager,*
    everything just seemed to fall into place. Now I've been
    given the sack and I don't know what to do. I don't even
    know what to feel about God. This seems a complete
    contradiction with what I thought God had promised me.'

Nothing significant began to happen to Abraham until he
was seventy-five. Prior to that, God had spoken to him in
Ur of the Chaldees where he lived, that's present day Iraq.
He listened to God and started moving not knowing
where he was heading. When he got to the place God had
in mind, God said, 'Look up into the sky. How many stars
can you see?' It doesn't tell us how Abraham responded
but he probably said, 'Lots, why?' 'Abraham, in this land
I'm going to give you as many descendants as the stars
you can see in the night's sky and as many descendants as
the grains of sand along the seashore. I'm going to give
you a son and from this son will come a nation and this
nation will be the means of blessing the world.'

Well, there were a few problems associated with that
promise. Abraham was seventy-five years old and his wife
was sixty-five. They'd been married for donkey's years
and they had no children – not for want of trying but the
Bible says 'She was barren.' Even if she hadn't been
barren, at sixty-five, she was long past the menopause.
And so, from every human point of view, what God was
telling Abraham was totally impossible. But the writer

says, in verse 11, 'he considered him faithful who made the promise.' Abraham must have said to himself, 'Well God, it's you who thought of this. I didn't think of this, I didn't ask you for this, you initiated this, you made the promise. And, if it's your idea, it's your promise, it is you who will bring it about. Thank you, I trust you.' His trust was credited to him as righteousness (Rom. 4:3).

● *Have you ever found yourself, like Abraham, in a situation that seemed totally impossible, yet at the same time convinced that God had brought you to this point? If appropriate, share your experiences with the group.*

Well, so far so good. What God didn't do, however, was to tell Sarah. Abraham had to go home and tell his wife. The Bible isn't complimentary about either Abraham or Sarah at this stage. It says about him in Hebrews 11:12 that he was 'as good as dead'. And in Genesis 18:12 it says Sarah was 'worn out'. Now I can imagine Abraham coming home, he's as good as dead, remember, and there's Sarah, all worn out, lying on the beanbag or wherever she used to lie. And Abraham saying, 'Sarah?' 'Yes?' 'God spoke to me today.' 'And what did he say?' 'You'll never, ever believe it, Sarah.' 'Go on, tell me.' 'He's going to give us something.' 'Oh, really, what's that?' 'It begins with B.' 'B, another beanbag?' 'No, not another beanbag, Sarah, he's going to give us a... a baby.' And the Bible says Sarah believed him. I think that's remarkable.

And the two of them waited, three months went by, six months went by, nine months went by. 'How are you feeling Sarah? Are you putting on weight? Are you getting sick in the mornings? Are you eating funny combinations?' One year went by, two years went by, five years went by, eight years went by, ten years went by and there was no baby. And one day, as Genesis 16 explains, Sarah brought the subject up. 'Abraham, are you sure God told you we're going to have a baby?' 'Well yes he did.' 'Are you sure it was God who told you that?' 'Well, yes, it was God who told me that.' 'Are you sure that wasn't the night you'd been eating some Danish Blue cheese and you, you know, had a strange dream?' 'No, no, it wasn't the cheese, God told me.' 'Well, where's the baby Abraham?' 'I don't know, Sarah, I've been wondering that myself, maybe God didn't know how worn out you were.' 'Maybe he didn't know how dead *you* were!'

The promise of God rang in their ears for ten years but there was no baby. The book of Hebrews, very kindly to Abraham, misses this next bit out because Abraham made the awful mistake of saying, 'I know God promised but it's not working so I had better do it for him.' And the couple made the arrangement that he would have the child through the maid, Hagar. It was part of the culture. We didn't invent surrogate motherhood; it's been around a long time. Hagar the maid gave birth to a son whom they called Ishmael. Abraham must have been thrilled and for the next fourteen years there was nothing more to worry about because they had their child. After fourteen years, when Abraham was ninety-nine years of age, that's twenty-four years after God had last spoken to him, God spoke again. 'Abraham?' 'Yes?' 'You remember I told you you'd have a son?' 'Yes.' 'This time next year your wife will give birth to a son.' And it says Abraham laughed, 'Can a man of a hundred father a son? Can a woman of ninety give birth to a son?' He went home and told Sarah and she laughed as well. But Genesis 21 tells us that Isaac was born on the very day God had said.

God is never in a hurry. We communicate so fast, we can just pick up a telephone and call across the world and speak to somebody else. We can get on a plane today, and we're anywhere in the world, by tomorrow. God doesn't work that way. It's interesting how God, throughout

Scripture, never seemed to be in a hurry. He told Eve that the seed of her womb would crush the head of the serpent. And when she gave birth to her first born son she said, 'I've gotten a man.' The force of the Hebrew is 'This is the promise.' They called him Cain. He wasn't 'the man' at all; he became a murderer. Generation after generation, century after century, millennium after millennium went by before there was a cry of a baby in Bethlehem. God takes his time.

Isaiah 5:19 has encouraged me enormously. The prophet gives a whole catalogue of woes, 'Woe to those who draw sin along with cords of deceit ...' 'Woe to those who are heroes at drinking wine ... Woe to those who call evil good and good evil.' We agree with him and then he says in verse 19, '(Woe) to those who say, "Let God hurry, let him hasten his work so that we may see it."' Isn't that interesting? You know God doesn't hurry.

- *When you want God to act immediately, what is this saying about:*
  - *Your view of God*
  - *Your view of yourself*
  - *Your view of faith*
- *What would you say to a Christian friend who said, 'I just wish that God would do something miraculous and intervene in this situation. We seem to lurch from crisis to crisis – if God did something wonderful it would make him look good. I'd be able to tell everyone how great God was.'*
- *What lessons could God be teaching you while you wait, while you persevere through a particular crisis or time of uncertainty?*

'Abraham, you're seventy-five years of age, Sarah is sixty-five, I'll give you a baby, I'll give you a son.' The logic is that as they're so old anyway, if God's going to act, he's going to do it now. You'd expect the baby in nine months, wouldn't you? But it's another twenty-five years before

Isaac's born. And once Isaac is born surely Abraham would expect him to grow up and have a family that would develop into this nation that God had promised. But, as Isaac grew up, it became obvious he wasn't very interested in girls. So when he was forty years old, Abraham employed a servant to find him a wife. The servant came back with a girl called Rebecca. Isaac said, 'She'll do.' And, of all the women in the world, of all the women in the Middle East, the Bible records 'Rebecca was barren.' Why didn't God pick a woman who was fertile? Why didn't he get Isaac married at the age of twenty, have a baby every year for the next twenty years and get this nation on the road? Instead he's forty before he finds a wife, she's barren and it's only after twenty years that she conceives and gives birth to twins: Jacob and Esau. Why didn't God get this thing moving? Why was it sixty-five years from the time God made the promise to Abraham, until the first grandchild came on the scene? God takes his time and we need to remember that when we get impatient.

God doesn't change; but he often works slowly. Abraham recognised this. Jesus said in John 8:56, 'Your father Abraham rejoiced at the thought of seeing my day; he saw it and was glad.' Abraham acknowledged, 'There's something going on here that's much bigger than Ishmael, much bigger than grandchildren, much bigger than great-grandchildren and God will take his time.' When we walk by faith, sometimes we do not know what God is doing; we have to wait. And God takes his time. Like Abraham, we need to trust God and say, 'God, you made a promise; the promise extends out for a long time but we trust you.'

Like Abraham, Moses was an old man when God called him. He was eighty years old when God met him at the burning bush. On that occasion everything God said to Moses was about himself, about God. You can read what the Lord said to Moses in Exodus 3:7-9:

> I have indeed seen the misery of my people in Egypt. I have
> heard them crying out because of their slave drivers, and I
> am concerned about their suffering. So I have come down to
> rescue them from the hand of the Egyptians...And now the
> cry of the Israelites has reached me, and I have seen the way
> the Egyptians are oppressing them.

Moses must have got very excited, 'God, at last, we have
been praying for this for years. You're going to do
something, wonderful. What are you going to do?' The
next verse says, 'So now, go. I'm sending you'. 'But I
thought you said you were going to do it.' 'Yes, Moses, I
will do it but I have to do it through you. You've got to
step out in obedience and you've got to trust me. Go back
to Pharaoh. I know you've been on the wanted list for
forty years after killing that Egyptian and I know,
humanly, the risk is he'll arrest you, but go.' So Moses
went and asked Pharaoh to release the Israelites. But
Pharaoh wasn't interested in Moses' request and refused.
Moses went back to God. 'What do I do now?' God said 'I
knew that would happen. Take your staff, Moses, hold it,
take it down to the river and just strike the water.' And, as
he did so, the water turned to blood. And the series of
plagues followed. At each stage, God sent the plagues and
Moses trusted him.

The final plague, the tenth plague was the death of
every first born in Egypt: the death of every first born male
in Egypt, of every first born lamb of every sheep in Egypt,
every first born calf of every cow in Egypt. And the
Israelites took a lamb that night and they slew it, they put
the blood on the doorposts of their homes and they
cooked it. They ate the meat, standing up, with their coats
on, their belts around their waists, their shoes on their feet,
their staffs in their hands, ready to run in the strength of
the lamb the moment the word came 'You're free.' And as

they left Egypt that morning there must have been a tremendous sense of relief. Their years of fear and oppression were over.

Trouble started when the people got to the Red Sea. Verse 29 says, 'By faith the people passed through the Red Sea as on dry land'. What does that mean? Exodus 14 tells us that when the Israelites got to the Red Sea, they couldn't cross it and so they began to grumble. When they looked over their shoulders and saw in the cloud of dust the silhouette of the Egyptian army, they realised that Pharaoh had changed his mind. He was coming to round them up and take them back to Egypt. The Red Sea hemmed them in, in front, and the Egyptian army hemmed them in behind and they began to panic. They complained to Moses, 'Was it because there were no graves in Egypt that you brought us to the desert to die? What have you done to us by bringing us out of Egypt? Didn't we say to you in Egypt, "Leave us alone; let us serve the Egyptians"? It would have been better for us to serve the Egyptians than to die in the desert!' (Ex. 14:11-12). I just love the way Moses answered them. 'Do not be afraid. Stand firm and you will see the deliverance the Lord will bring you today... The Lord will fight for you; you need only to be still' (Ex. 14:13-14).

Now how can Moses speak like that? The Red Sea was too wide to bridge, too deep to tunnel under, too long to go around and the Egyptians were gaining from behind. Moses probably prayed very quickly and said, 'God, we've got a problem, in fact we got two; a Red Sea in front of us, an Egyptian army behind us. I don't know how we can possibly get out of this situation but I want to remind you of something: it wasn't my idea to come. You called me and when you sent me, you said, "I will be with you." So I said, "What is your name?" and you said, "I am who I am. That is in the present tense, in any situation, I am totally sufficient in any crisis, I am. You know I was the one at the burning bush, the one who called you, remember you're called and that'll keep you motivated. I will be the one in Canaan to welcome you when you get there but I am, in the present tense, Moses, everything you'll ever need, at any time, in any crisis, when your back's against any wall, I am, present tense." So you told me we're going to Canaan, this is only the border of Egypt. Humanly there is no hope for us but it's your business so I trust you. Amen.'

● *How can we be more like Moses and instinctively turn to God in faith when we see a crisis looming?*

Isn't it great to talk to God like that, when you know God has put you in a situation and everything around seems to be folding in? Moses could turn to the people and say, 'Don't be afraid, relax, quit the panic, the Lord will fight for you; you only have to be still.' That didn't mean they just stood on the banks and said 'Well, let's just wait for God to do something.' No, God told them to keep moving. Perhaps Moses had a gentle discussion with God, 'All right, I'll go as far as I can, I'll put my toe in the water, now what?' 'Take your staff, hold your staff over the sea.' Moses held his staff over the sea all night. I'm sure it was slightly embarrassing in the midst of all this panic and complaints for God's leader to stand by the sea with his staff. It was hardly the strategy you'd expect from a dynamic leader. I'm sure all kinds of rumours went around: 'You know, he's got a piece of string on the end of that staff, with a hook on it.' But Moses learnt that you obey what God says and you trust who God is. Obedience and dependency are like two wings on an aircraft, you cannot separate them. When the morning broke the next morning, there was a path through the sea and they went through on dry ground.

● *'Moses learnt that you obey what God says and you trust who God is.' What is it about God that keeps you trusting in him?*

Moses learnt that faith sees beyond circumstances. It was as if God said to Moses, 'I know that from every human point of view this is a totally impossible assignment I'm giving you, to take these people through to Canaan, through the wilderness. But Moses, it's I who's going to be the source, trust me.' And the writer of Hebrews says 'by faith Moses crossed the Red Sea'.

Faith sees beyond circumstances. I wonder what circumstances you're in, right now? In good conscience before God, you have sought his direction. And, by the way, he has actually promised to us that if we acknowledge him in all our ways, he will direct our paths. You don't have to say, 'Lord, guide me today', every day; just acknowledge him and he'll guide you as he promised. You don't always know, 'Why has he put me where I am?' Just trust him. Sometimes you're in the will of God and you're trusting him for his will and purpose and yet things seem to go wrong. You step out in obedience and everything begins to collapse in front of you; you're not the first to have been there, at all. But faith sees beyond circumstances. God is going to fulfil his purpose.

● *Why does God allow us to be in situations where we're in his will but everything seems to go wrong?*

● *Hebrews 11 says 'By faith Abraham ...' 'By faith Moses ...' Insert your name into this list, 'By faith ...' How would you want the sentence to end, what do you want to be remembered for?*

FURTHER STUDY
What other examples are there in the Old and New Testaments of believers having to wait patiently on God? What insights does this give you into God's big picture and his plans for us?

REFLECTION AND RESPONSE

Reflect on the different facets of your life. Where can you see God's fingerprints? Talk with someone else in the group about where God is asking you to have a faith that sees beyond circumstances. Explain whether you think God wants you to have a faith that waits like Abraham's or a faith that moves forward like Moses'. As you pray, lay hands on each other to affirm that God's fingerprints are all over your life, even if you can't see them now.

CHAPTER 10

Faith sees beyond character and conflict

Aim: Trusting God despite our failings and through our suffering

Read: Hebrews 11:1-40
Key verses: Hebrews 11:30-40

Faith sees beyond character. If I were to ask you what is the most important, somebody's faith or their character, you might well say their character. Character is important because the goal of the Lord Jesus Christ, in your life and mine, is to conform us to the image of Christ and therefore there is change of character. The fruit of the Spirit can be summed up in one word: character. But I want to show you, from Hebrews 11, that there are people whose character, as far as we know, never really developed but who lived by faith. You see it's possible to be good but useless; or to be underdeveloped in character, yet bold in faith. Here are two examples: Rahab and Samson.

You can find the full story of Rahab in Joshua 2. I doubt very much, if I was writing the Letter to the Hebrews, that I would include Rahab in this list of heroes of faith. She was a prostitute and a liar. You may remember, when Joshua was about to enter the land of Canaan, he sent two spies in just to check everything out. These spies found lodging in the house of Rahab. Her house was an obvious choice because it was not unusual for strange men to stay with Rahab. Their being there didn't arouse too much suspicion, because prostitution trades in anonymity. Then the king of Jericho heard rumours there were spies in Rahab's house so he sent a message to her, 'Bring out the men who came to you and entered your house, because they have come to spy out the whole land.' But Rahab had hidden the spies, it says, and she reported, 'Yes, the men came to me, (but) I did not know where they had come from. At dusk, when it was time to close the city gate, the men left. I don't know which way they went. Go after them quickly. You may catch up with them.' Now that was just a big fib. I'm sorry but it was. Because the next verse says, in brackets, 'But she had taken them up to the roof and hidden them under the stalks of flax she had laid out on the roof.'

So Rahab got these spies off the hook by deceit. No doubt, of course, lying was par for the course for Rahab. I'm sure there are many, many times when suspicious wives came knocking on her door and inquiring, 'Has so and so been here?' 'Oh no, no, no, no, I've never seen him.' Lying must have been commonplace in Rahab's line of work. So why is she commended for her faith? Joshua 2:9 reports Rahab's words to the spies: she said 'I know that the Lord has given this land to you'. That's past tense; she knew that God had already given Jericho into the hands of the Israelites. She's heard the Lord had dried up the water of the Red Sea for them forty years ago; people were still talking about it. She'd also heard how the Israelites had destroyed Sihon and Og, the two kings of the Amorites east of the Jordan, a few weeks ago. She's saying, 'Listen, I know God *has* given this land to you. Do you know why I know that? Because we've heard the stories of what happened forty years ago, what happened a few weeks ago and we know that your God is *the* God. And the day we heard that there was a nomadic tribe coming across the desert, heading for this city, we knew our days were numbered. Not because of you, you're just a nomadic tribe of people but because of your God.'

The spies replied 'Our lives for your lives! ... If you don't tell what we are doing, we will treat you kindly and faithfully when the Lord gives us the land.' (Josh. 2:15) Rahab had spoken with past tense certainty: 'the Lord has given this land to you.' The spies replied 'when the Lord gives us the land', speaking in the future tense with a touch of uncertainty. This explains why the writer to the Hebrews included Rahab in his list of faith. Yes, she was a prostitute; yes, she was messed up in all kinds of ways. And a lot of people are messed up for reasons that, if you understood them, you would be extremely sympathetic with. There are all kinds of reasons why people's lives are messed up but out of her mess she said, 'I know that your God is the true God.' You can be a good-living person but never trust God. You can be theologically informed and doctrinally correct but sterile. No doubt these spies had a better theology than Rahab did. They would have known the law. They would have seen the establishment of the tabernacle in the wilderness. They would have known its message about the holiness of God, about the sinfulness of humanity, about the need for atonement and the shedding of the blood of innocent animals as a substitute for the people. They knew all the theology, Rahab knew none of it, all she knew was this: 'Your God is alive.'

- *When have new believers like Rahab shown up your lack of faith?*
- *How can we make sure our theology and teaching help us trust God rather than getting in the way?*

Many of us still have a lurking sense that we need to earn God's approval; that we need to dot our I's and cross our T's if God is going to bless us and work with us and in us. But the marvellous thing is, as Hebrews 11:6 says, 'Without faith it is impossible to please God'. So the reverse is true 'With faith, it's impossible not to please God.' When God saw Rahab's dependency on him he said, 'I love that woman, she's a woman through whom I'll work.' You know that Rahab became the great-great-grandmother of King David? God led her on, brought her in, she became one of the Israelites, and as a proselyte to Israel. Her life was saved by hanging a scarlet cord from her window, letting the Israelites know not to take her house when they took the city. There are some who say, 'I've got all these things in my life that I know are wrong. I've got this persistent sin I seem unable to cope with.' And there may be all kinds of reasons why you can't cope with it but God will still use you, if you say, 'Lord, I'm going to trust you.' Stop trying to look for other ways to get God's blessing, just have the faith that says, 'God, I take you at your word and I just trust you.'

- *Why do you think we try to earn God's approval and blessing rather than just relying on him like Rahab?*

Another guy who messed up was Samson. Samson's given a lot of space in the Bible: there's more attention given to him than to any other judge. Here in Hebrews 11 he's just mentioned by name but he has a fascinating story. He was born to a barren mother. His birth had been announced by an angel, which puts him in the league of Isaac and John the Baptist. He was to be a Nazarite, from birth, which meant he was to take certain vows not to drink wine, eat grapes or raisins, go near a dead body or cut his hair. And he broke all those vows. His big problem was his promiscuity; he fell easily in and out of love with women. He fell in love with Delilah, a prostitute in Gaza, and he foolishly told her the secret of his strength. Eventually he was captured by the Philistines: they gouged out his eyes and locked him up. And, locked up in his cell, his hair began to grow again and God restored his strength. Samson became the first suicide terrorist. He went to the temple and prayed, 'God, just one time, give me strength' and he pushed against the pillars of the temple. He killed more people when he died than while he was alive and he killed quite a few while he lived. What is redeemable about that story? What's good is there in it? The whole story of Samson is tragic and yet five times we read that the Spirit of the Lord came upon him in power. Despite all his weaknesses and failings, Hebrews 11 says this was a man who trusted God.

● *What do the stories of Rahab and Samson teach us about God's view of failure? How does this affect how you think of your own and other people's failings?*

Faith sees beyond character, faith is actually more important than character. Certainly we need to grow in character and godliness. But we need to give as much attention to the question, 'Am I really trusting God in every area of my life?' When God writes biographies, he writes them differently to the way we do. God doesn't see us as other people see us. He doesn't look at our outward appearance that may have fallen apart for all kinds of reasons. God looks at our heart. Do you know what kind of heart he's looking for? 2 Chronicles 16:9 tells us 'the eyes of the Lord run to and fro, throughout the whole earth, to show himself strong on the behalf of those whose heart is perfect towards him' (Authorised Version). The eyes of the Lord are running all over the place, looking for somebody who will let God show himself strong on their behalf. He's not looking for men and women who will show themselves strong for God. He's looking for people who allow God to show himself strong in them. He's looking for women like Rahab who said, 'God will give you the land.' 'Thank you, Rahab, you're a lady who will trust me to show myself strong.' He's looking for men like Samson who, despite all the mess, cried 'God, give me strength.' 'Thank you Samson, even against these stone pillars you trust me to show myself strong.' Is God strong in your life? It's not that character doesn't matter, of course it matters, but faith is more important than character.

● *In what area of your life does God want to show himself strong? Are you allowing a past or present failing to get in the way of God acting?*

This next section Hebrews 11:32-40 is a difficult passage to read but I'm so glad it is in this chapter.

> And what more shall I say? I do not have time to tell about Gideon, Barak, Samson, Jephthah, David, Samuel and the prophets, who through faith conquered kingdoms, administered justice, and gained what was promised; who shut the mouths of lions, quenched the fury of the flames, and escaped the edge of the sword; whose weakness was turned to strength; and who became powerful in battle and routed foreign armies. Women received back their dead, raised to life again. Others were tortured and refused to be

released, so that they might gain a better resurrection. Some faced jeers and flogging, while still others were chained and put in prison. They were stoned; they were sawn in two; they were put to death by the sword. They went about in sheepskins and goatskins, destitute, persecuted and ill-treated – the world was not worthy of them. They wandered in deserts and mountains, and in caves and holes in the ground. These were all commended for their faith, yet none of them received what had been promised. God had planned something better for us so that only together with us would they be made perfect'.

We might be forgiven for assuming from the earlier verses that faith in God always leads to recognised success, ultimately. We might assume that, ultimately, we're never beaten, we're not overcome, and we don't really get hurt but that's not true. The writer to the Hebrews gives examples of people commended for their faith who died, were persecuted and who suffered. Please don't get the idea that if you have faith in God you'll avoid all the hardships in life; that you'll never get sick, you'll never get down, you'll never be depressed, and you'll never be hurt.

Stephen was the first martyr recorded in the books of Acts. You've probably noticed that when Stephen was being crushed to death by these stones, he looked up and saw Jesus, standing at the right hand of the Father. This is interesting because Jesus is normally never standing at the right hand of the Father; he's normally seated at the right hand of the Father. Some have said he was standing to welcome the first martyr home, well maybe. But the point is that although Stephen saw Jesus standing at the right hand of the Father, he didn't lift a finger to help Stephen. Jesus let Stephen's body be crushed to death, he let the stones break his bones and probably his skull and he watched him die. Jesus saw Stephen's blood-soaked face and he didn't rescue him. Jesus knew; 'Stephen, this is tough for you, very tough for you, but I'm planting a seed. See that young man over there, looking after those coats, his name's Saul of Tarsus, he's the arch enemy of the church.' Later Saul became a Christian, he changed his name to Paul and he began to preach. If you study the sermons of Paul, in the book of Acts, and the sermons of Peter in the book of Acts, they preach very differently, but, interestingly, the style of Paul is identical to the style of Stephen. God allowed the death of Stephen because he had a plan; he was sowing seeds in Saul of Tarsus that day.

● *Men like Stephen and the others in the list of faith were 'commended for their faith, yet none of them received what had been promised' (Heb. 11:39). What does it mean to be 'commended' by God?*

● *The people in Hebrews 11 did not see the outcome of their faith; they didn't receive what had been promised because God was still sowing the seeds. What was his ultimate plan? What does Hebrews 11:40 mean for them and for us?*

Major Chhirc Taing came to the Keswick convention in 1973. I knew Chhirc because he came to Glasgow for a year to study the Bible when I was a student at the same college. He had a room just near mine, and I got to know him. At the end of that year he went back to Cambodia and he said, 'I know my life is in danger if I go back.' He'd been a major in the Cambodian army, he was a man in his thirties. 'If I go back I know I'm in danger but I must go back, God is telling me to go.' And he went back and within a few months he was martyred and the soldiers that killed him washed and cleaned their boots in his blood. You can read his story in *Killing Fields, Living Fields.*[1]

I was in China last year and I visited one of the well-known leaders of a house church. I went to his three-storey house, and every room was jammed, packed with chairs. I may be taller than the average Chinaman but I couldn't put my knees anywhere between them. On the top floor is a small room where there's a television camera and he would preach to this camera, and the message was relayed to every floor and every room in the house. The man lived very simply; he only had a bed he pulled down from the wall to sleep on at night. And yet three thousand people in about six or seven different services came into that church, or rather that house, each weekend. We sat and talked together. He told me that he'd spent more than twenty years in jail. He said, 'When we first started thirty people used to meet in my home and they arrested me and put me in prison for two years. At the end of those two years, when I came back, there were two hundred people in my home.' He said, 'Hallelujah! Persecution is good.' I can't say that but he said that. He said, 'After a while, they arrested me again, they put me back in jail for three years. When I came back, after three years, there were eight hundred people in my home. Hallelujah! Persecution is good. And, after a while, they took me away again, they kept me in jail for fifteen years. When I came back, there were three thousand people in my home.' He said, 'Persecution is good.' I can't say that, of course, because I know nothing about that, I'm just telling you what he said. But he bore, on his body, the marks of his persecution. By faith he went to jail for more than twenty years. By faith maltreated, by faith whipped, scourged but three thousand people, and probably more now, meet in his home every week. You see, faith sees beyond conflict, faith sees beyond disaster.

● *How is Jesus an example to us of faith that perseveres through suffering and sees beyond apparent disasters?*

We live in a very comfortable environment. No one's going to come and raid your home and lock you up; we've got enough food to eat, the temperature's comfortable. But you know God, again and again, does his best work when people have exhausted their human resources. These characters in Hebrews 11 didn't escape conflict and tragedies but they persevered through them by faith. Some were sawn in two, others thrown to the lions but they were men and women of faith. In our normal sphere of work and life, we're going to see God act. We'll be able to please God by our faith. Without faith it's impossible to please him. If we're going to please God, then we're going to be folks who have a faith that sees beyond circumstances and a faith that sees beyond character; so don't write anybody off. Look for that spark of a disposition of trust in God; he will look after their character if they are trusting him. And develop a faith that sees beyond conflicts. If without faith it's impossible to please God, then the reverse is also true – with faith it's impossible not to please God. You can go to bed at night and say, 'Today may have been a tough day, today may have been a hard day, today may be a day I would not like to live through again; what I do know is God has been pleased because I've lived today in dependency on him, trusting him to work out his purpose. Faith is being sure of what we hope for. It may not be in my hand now but I know that God is going to bring about his work, he's going to accomplish his purpose.' Will you trust him like this?

● *What has Hebrews reminded you about faith that will help you deal with the difficulties you are going through? Be specific.*

FURTHER STUDY

Hebrews 11:32 commends Gideon, Barak, Jephthah, David and Samuel. What particular aspects of their faith do you think they were commended for? Look for answers in Hebrews 11:33-38 and reread their stories in the Old Testament to give you some ideas. What do their examples teach us about faith and the type of people God uses?

REFLECTION AND RESPONSE

Think back to the 'Focus on the theme' at the beginning of this chapter. In the light of your own situation, come up with a personal definition of faith. What does it mean for you to have faith in God now? Write down your statement – 'Faith is...' Keep this declaration in your Bible as a reminder to you or give it to another friend in the group and ask them to encourage you to keep your faith.

REVIEW OF HEBREWS 11:1-40

Reread the chapter of faith. What is God saying to you about your faith in him?

- Is it difficult to see God's hand-print on your life and do you need faith beyond circumstances?
- Have you failed God and do you need to be reminded that he looks for faith beyond character?
- Is life full of hardship and do you need to have faith beyond conflict?

Hebrews 11 brings up many big issues that we need to grapple with but perhaps most of us just need to get back to basics and ask 'Did I bring God pleasure today? How can I bring him more pleasure tomorrow?'

POINTS TO PONDER

- What have you learnt about God?
- What have you learnt about yourself?
- What actions or attitudes do you need to change as a result?

---

[1] Don Cormack, *Killing Fields, Living Fields* (Monarch, 2001)

CHAPTER 11

Looking back to God's sufficiency

Aim: Learning from the heroes of faith

FOCUS ON THE THEME
How well do you know the past?
- Do you like looking at old photos and videos?
- Would you choose to watch a black and white film?
- When is the last time you went to a museum?
- What grade did you get for your history exams at school?
- Have you studied your family tree?

You may not be a history buff but make an exception when it comes to your faith! Studying the past helps us make sense of the present and gives us confidence for the future.

Read: Hebrews 12:1-13
Key verse: Hebrews 12:1

The moment we come into union with Christ, repent and place our faith in him, we begin a journey that will culminate, of course, only when we get to heaven. Then we will fully enjoy all the provision God has for us. But, in the meantime, we're on a journey to maturity. Hebrews 6:1-6 explains that there are two options in the Christian life: you either go on to maturity or you subject the Son of God to public disgrace. What you cannot do, if you fall away, is 'be brought back to repentance' (v6) which, as the writer has earlier stated, means you cannot return to 'the foundation of repentance' (v1). Repentance is the foundation of the Christian life, but you cannot return to your pre-saved state and start all over again. If you do 'fall away', as it is impossible to go back to your pre-saved state, instead you 'subject Christ to public disgrace' (v6). The only alternative therefore is to 'go on to maturity' (v1) which is the appeal of chapter 6, taken up throughout the book and again here in chapter 12.

So how do we press on to maturity? The writer to the Hebrews in chapter 12 encourages us to look in four directions. First of all, we are to *look back*. Now, let me tell you why I say that. Verse 1 says 'since we are surrounded by such a great cloud of witnesses,' the folks he's been describing and explaining in chapter 11, 'let us throw off everything that hinders and the sin that so easily entangles and (let us) run with perseverance the race marked out for us.' The writer urges us to look back at 'this great cloud of witnesses'. It's not that people like Noah, Abraham, Isaac, Moses and Samuel are spectators looking through the clouds saying, 'How they doing this morning? Some of them really need moving on.' Rather it is that the experience of God in the lives of these people, throughout the history of Israel, are witnesses to us of God's sufficiency in our times of need. If you're facing a big problem, go back to Abraham; how does your problem compare with Abraham's? What did Abraham do? If you're facing a crisis, go back to Moses. What did Moses do by faith? What can you do by faith and how can you depend on the resources that Moses enjoyed? You can go back to Noah and all these men, they are all witnesses to Christ, they're witnesses to the sufficiency of God in their lives.

● *Who is your favourite Bible character? How does their example inspire you?*

● *Think back through the stories of Abraham, Moses and Noah. Brainstorm how each of these characters witnessed the sufficiency of God.*

In effect, the writer is saying to us, 'Listen, you're not the first one on this journey, you're not the first one to face these troubles, you're not the first one to face these temptations and crises. I've given you this catalogue of just some of the people in the olden days who knew God. They are witnesses to us that our God, "Jesus Christ is the same yesterday and today and for ever"' (Heb. 13:8).

It's easy to look back and get nostalgic about the good old days, isn't it? The good old days are usually the result of either a bad memory or a good imagination or a combination of both. It says in Ecclesiastes, 'Do not say "why were the old days better than these?" … (for) it is not wise to ask such questions.' 'The good old days' of chapter 11 were actually the tough old days. God does his best work in tough situations. We discover the sufficiency of God most when we're exhausted. A friend of mine, Ron Dunn, who died recently, once said a wonderful thing, 'You do not know that Jesus Christ is all you need, until Christ is all you've got. When Christ is all you've got, then you realise that Christ is all you need.' It's true, isn't it?

These characters from the chapter of faith were involved in constant battle. 'Their God is our God,' the writer says, 'we're surrounded by these witnesses of the sufficiency of God.' Therefore we need to 'throw off everything that hinders and the sin that so easily entangles.' This 'throwing off' – it's not something we hear a lot of preaching about these days, because we want to be positive. And ninety nine per cent of the gospel is positive; in fact it's all positive. But I want you to know that self-denial is every bit a part of Christian experience, as living in the fullness of God. Taking up the cross is as much a part of the Christian life as enjoying his resurrection life.

Brokenness is God's agenda for us as a prelude to wholeness. Dying with Christ is necessary that we might live with him. Too often we want the positives without the negatives, we want the benefits without the obligations.

● *What will our Christian experience be like if we don't 'throw off' sin, if we don't take up the cross and embrace brokenness?*

And this chapter talks about the things you've got to throw off. Let's look at just one example from the life of Moses. In 11:24-25 it says

> By faith Moses, when he had grown up, refused to be known as the son of Pharaoh's daughter. He chose to be ill-treated along with the people of God rather than to enjoy the pleasures of sin for a short time. He regarded disgrace for the sake of Christ as of greater value than the treasures of Egypt, because he was looking ahead to his reward.

The Bible says that he refused to be known as the son of Pharaoh's daughter. Having been adopted into the royal family of one of the greatest nations on earth, all the privileges of such position were laid at Moses' feet but he denied himself those privileges. Not because they were, in themselves, intrinsically wrong but because they would interfere with God's purpose for him. That's why Hebrews makes this analogy of running the race. If you're going to run a race there's nothing wrong with big boots but you don't wear them when you run a race. There's nothing wrong with a thick, heavy coat, but you don't wear it if you have any intention of reaching the finishing line. And there are things in life that are not intrinsically wrong; whether they are right or wrong is not the issue. The issue is 'What enables me to further God's interest, God's purpose, God's agenda in my life?' Because that which hinders his agenda, that which blocks his purpose, that which impedes my growth in holiness, may not be wrong for somebody else but it needs to come out of my life.

- *What did characters such as Abraham and Noah 'throw off'?*
- *What have you denied yourself, not because it was intrinsically wrong but because it would interfere with God's plan for your life?*

To press on to spiritual maturity, Moses denied himself the pleasures of sin and sin is pleasurable. I don't go along with people who say, 'Sin is just terrible.' It's fun actually, that's why we have a problem with it. I mean by definition temptation is attractive, otherwise it wouldn't be a temptation, would it? For an example I'm never tempted to walk in front of a moving bus. It's not attractive to me. I don't struggle with that issue. But I am tempted, sometimes, to push somebody else in front of a moving bus. By definition, every temptation I face is only a temptation because, deep in my heart, I think 'If I could get away with this; if this didn't matter, if nobody knew, if God couldn't see, I would do it.' And if you're like me, you struggle with temptation every day of your life because sin is attractive. That's why we've got to live beyond, simply, what feels good; we've got to live beyond satisfying our senses. The motto of our day is 'If it feels good, do it.'

Moses had that option, he could have enjoyed all the pleasures of sin. I don't know what kind of pleasures of sin the writer was talking about but you can be sure that growing up in the royal palace of Pharaoh, he could click his fingers and get almost anything he wanted. Any girl he wanted, he could probably get. But he recognised that pleasure was for a season and he recognised he was in life for the long-term. You're not here for the season, you're here for the long-term. And he chose instead to be ill-treated and take his place with the people of God.

- *Brainstorm what Christians are tempted by.*
- *How can we gain the strength to avoid these temptations and 'throw off' sin?*

He wasn't just ill-treated by the Egyptians. Remember it was because of Moses that Pharaoh made the Israelites make bricks without straw. Without straw the bricks would just crumble. The people were upset and complained to Moses, 'May the Lord look upon you and judge you! You have made us a stench to Pharaoh and his officials and have put a sword in their hand to kill us' (Ex. 5:21). Moses was misunderstood by his own people. 'You've upset Pharaoh; it's been the policy to work with the Egyptians, it least that gives us the best possible deal and you've messed it up.' So he didn't just choose to be ill treated with the people of God, he chose to be ill-treated by the people of God. Sometimes, when you pursue the goal you know God has given to you or the goal you find in his word, you are sometimes mistreated by the people of God. Persecution doesn't just come from the outside, persecution comes from inside and you may well be facing that. It's always good to listen to other people's perspective and find out if they're right or not, but it's important to go back to the word of God and say, 'If this is what God has told me, if this is what his word says, if this is how his Spirit is leading me, I press on even though the people of God don't understand.' This is what Moses did.

- *How do you cope with ill-treatment from the people of God? Does Moses' example offer any encouragement?*

Moses 'regarded disgrace for the sake of Christ as of greater value than the treasures of Egypt because he was looking ahead to his reward' (Heb. 11:26). He was looking ahead. And, in fact, if you go through chapter 11 carefully you'll notice this idea of looking ahead occurs a number of times. Verse 10: Abraham 'was looking forward to the city

with foundations, whose architect and builder is God.'
Verse 16: 'they were longing for a better country – a
heavenly one.' Verse 40: 'God had planned something
better for us so that only together with us would they be
made perfect.' The writer is saying 'Press on to maturity,
keep looking forward to your ultimate reward. Listen,
throw off these things that bog you down, that pull you
down because you're pushing on to an objective that'll be
hindered by this. And especially the sin which so easily
entangles us because sin is so seductive.'

Chapter 12 illustrates one of the sins that trap us easily.
Verse 16 says 'See that no-one is sexually immoral, or is
godless like Esau, who for a single meal sold his
inheritance rights as the oldest son.' You probably think
sex is the big temptation to avoid but do you know in the
Bible, food is actually the big one. Look in the Garden of
Eden: when Eve saw the fruit was good for food, she took
it and ate it. Esau, for a plate of food, lost his birthright.
The Israelites, in the wilderness, wanted to go back into
Egypt. Why? The food. 'The manna, we're sick of this
manna, manna for breakfast, manna for lunch, manna for
supper. Let's go back to Egypt, there we sat around pots of
meat and ate garlic and onions and cucumbers and melons
and leeks.'

● *Why do we not talk very much about food being one of the*
  sins that trap us?

Isn't it interesting the very first attack on Jesus was this,
'Turn these stones to bread.' Food is a big problem in the
Bible and the writer associates food with sexual
immorality here. They are similar because they're
appetites we've not learned to control, or we've learned to
satisfy illegitimately. As a pastor, I'm discovering that one
of the biggest problems that men are facing is Internet
pornography. In the past two years, I've talked to a

number of couples who are wanting to separate and this has been an ingredient in every single case. If you are prone to this temptation, you'd better get some help because it becomes literally addictive. It will entangle you. It's not the biggest sin in the world, of course, and it's actually one of the easiest sins to understand, simply because we have sexual appetites.

Whatever area your particular sin may be, whatever your particular vulnerability may be, look back to this great cloud of witnesses, and remind yourself, 'Their God is my God, their God was adequate for them, he is adequate for me. He's Jesus, the same yesterday, today and for ever.'

● *In what particular area of your life do you need to be reminded of God's sufficiency? How does this great cloud of witnesses help spur you on?*

FURTHER STUDY

Looking back to our own past or to the experience of others helps remind us of God's faithfulness and his sufficiency for all our needs. In what ways did the Old Testament characters draw strength from looking at the past? For example, how did looking back to the past help David keep trusting in God?

REFLECTION AND RESPONSE

God made us to love him and serve him but what in particular did he have in mind when he created you? What purpose did he have in mind for you? Think about your gifts, talents, interests; what keeps you talking late into the night? Then write a single sentence summary of what you consider your purpose to be. You might have to do a few drafts! Take into account that your purpose will probably change throughout the different phases of your life. Once you've got a purpose statement, think:

- What sin do I need to 'throw off' to help me fulfil this purpose?
- What legitimate things do I need to 'throw off' to help me fulfil this purpose?
- What hurtful comments from God's own people do I need to put aside?
- How has God's faithfulness in the past encouraged me to keep pursuing this goal?
- What inspiration do the heroes of the faith offer me?
- How can those around me help me run my particular race with perseverance?

Spend time praising God together for the people who have motivated you to keep running the Christian race – it could be members of your congregation, your Sunday school teacher, the author of a book which inspired you or a speaker you once heard. Pray for each other that you, too, would be an example to others of someone who had run the race well. Pray that as the next generation looks back, your life would be one that inspires them.

Look up to Christ

Aim: Learning to keep our focus on Christ

FOCUS ON THE THEME
What has been the main focus of your attention this past year?
• Moving house
• Transitioning to retirement
• Health problems
• An important work project
• Your children
• Other

With so many legitimate issues that vie for our attention we need to consider how we deal with them all and at the same time maintain our focus on Christ.

Read: Hebrews 12:1-13
Key verses: Hebrews 12:2-13

If we are to press on to maturity the second direction we need to *look* is *up*. Verse 2 says, 'Let us fix our eyes on Jesus, the author and perfecter of our faith, who for the joy set before him endured the cross'. I know Jesus isn't necessarily 'up'. Of course Jesus lives within us and there is a sense in which he is on the right hand of the Father in heaven. But I think you'll agree when we look up to the highest possible peak of the universe, we look to Christ. Just raise your eyes, look up.

The context is this catalogue of faith and the writer says 'Jesus is the author and he's the finisher of our faith.' In other words, faith is as valued as the object in which it is placed. You put a lot of faith in thin ice, you'll step onto the thin ice but you'll sink by faith because, although your faith is plenty, the ice is weak. Faith never makes up for the weakness of the object. If faith is an analogy of trust in an object, the object in whom we place our faith is Christ. He's the one, the author, the beginner, he doesn't just leave us there, he goes on as the one in whom we place our trust. And if we're going to grow and mature in the Christian life we don't move beyond Christ but every day we live in that dependency on Christ. That's why back in chapter 3:1, the writer says, 'Fix your thoughts on Jesus,' and here in chapter 12:2, 'Fix our eyes on Jesus'. Because it follows that the more you know Christ, the more you fix your attention on him, the more you're going to trust him. The reason why we don't trust God is, very simply, we don't know him well enough. And the more we get to know him, the more easy it becomes to trust him. That's why we fix our eyes on Christ.

- *Given your stage of life, how do you fix your thoughts and eyes on Christ?*
  - *Have you found a suitable study guide to help you in your daily Bible reading?*
  - *What helps you remember Jesus thoughout the day?*
  - *How do you maintain your concentration when you pray?*
  - *Do you find meditation and memorising Bible verses useful?*
- *Can you think of a more common expression or a visual image to describe Jesus' role in our faith rather than 'author and perfecter'?*

By the way, the more confident we are in the object of our faith, the less conscious we become of the exercise of our faith. Let me illustrate this. Just suppose somebody was to drive from Keswick to Istanbul. It's a long way, more than a thousand miles, and you have a choice of travelling in a 1965 Volkswagen Beetle or a brand new Bentley. Let me suggest to you, if you chose to go in the Volkswagen Beetle, you could be pretty sure somebody would say to you, 'Man, you must have a lot of faith.' Why? I'll tell you why: because they're not confident in the car. But if you were to choose the brand new Bentley, it's likely nobody would say, 'Wow, you must have a lot of faith.' Because the more confident you are in the object of your faith, the less conscious you become of the exercise of your faith. It becomes a natural, daily thing. That's why, when we stand back in amazement at somebody's great faith and say, 'Wow, man, they've got a lot of faith', what we're really saying is, 'I don't think too much of their God because they're willing to trust him. Boy, they're going to take some big risks. I'm impressed.' Does that make sense? So one of the most important things in the Christian life is to get to know God, to get to know Christ. That's why we read the word of God, not to get to know the Bible because that would makes us Pharisees, but to get to know Christ. We get to know God as we experience him in tough times and difficulties. The more confident we become in Christ, the less conscious we become of any risk element, because we're so confident in him.

- *What people or things do you have trouble entrusting to Christ and why?*
- *If we're confident in Christ, why do we still get anxious about things?*

Why do we look to Jesus? We look to Christ because even he was oriented towards the future. Why did he endure the cross? And I'm interested that the writer says, 'Actually, he endured the cross.' We know that Christ went willingly to the cross, but don't ever get the idea he went waltzing to the cross and said, 'Oh well, this is all par for the course.' We know in the Garden of Gethsemane he said, 'Father, if it's possible for this cup to be taken from me, if there's any other way that a man, a woman, a boy or a girl can be reconciled to a holy God; if there's any other way, please let that be the way; but if there is no other way, your will be done.' But he went to the cross, he endured the cross, it was agony, we can't begin to understand that. We might speculate about the physical agony, though we can't really, but we can't even begin to understand the spiritual agony of crying, 'My God, why have you forsaken me?' The very atmosphere of hell descended on him in those hours of darkness. Why did he do it? For the joy set before him. You see, why do we live this way? Because we're orientated to a future, we're orientated to something yet to be. We pay the price now in order that we may share that glory.

- *What did it mean for Jesus to be forsaken by God?*
- *Why do we lose focus on Christ? What gets in the way of remembering that the joy is primarily before us in heaven rather than here on earth?*

In the prophetic statement in Isaiah 53 about the cross, we read that Jesus 'saw the travail of his soul and was satisfied.' It tells you how much he loves you and me. What was the joy set before him? You and I, we were the joy set before him; the joy of knowing human beings might be redeemed and reconciled to God. So, says the writer, if you want to mature, look back at this great cloud of witnesses, look up to Jesus the author and the finisher of your faith who for the joy set before him endured the cross. You get your focus on the future, as he focused on the future.

- *Jesus' aim is that we all become mature believers. How can we help people to attain this goal? Consider the following scenarios:*

- *Your friend's daughter became a Christian as a young child but became less interested in church in her teenage years and now she's at university, she's rebelled completely. Is there anything her family and friends can do to help or is this just one of the decisions she has to make on her own?*

- *A young mother who came to the Mother and Toddler group at church recently attended an Alpha course. She has become a Christian but what is next? How can the church and individual members help her grow in her new faith?*

- *You have a group of mature Christian friends. You all know the Bible well and go to Christian conferences together. How can you encourage a deeper level of friendship where you actually spur one another on in your faith?*

FURTHER STUDY

Explore these terms 'fix' and 'set' further. Look up in the NIV Deuteronomy 11:18, Psalm 141:8, Romans 8:5, 2 Corinthians 4:18, Colossians 3:1-2, 1 Peter 1:13. What more do you learn about where and how we are to fix/set our thoughts and minds?

REFLECTION AND RESPONSE

Spend time together praising Jesus for who he is. Focus on the names and roles of Jesus and what they mean to you – healer, deliverer, rock, shepherd, for example. To help maintain your focus do something different in your worship time – perhaps kneel or stand up. Being more conscious of what you are doing will help you concentrate.

With your focus now on Jesus, think back to the issue you discussed in the 'Focus on the theme' section. See the issue which has consumed your time and energy through the eyes of Jesus: view it knowing you can act in his strength, pray about it and then leave it with him. Don't be anxious but rest in him.

CHAPTER 13

Looking beyond our suffering

Aim: To recognise how God uses suffering in our lives

FOCUS ON THE THEME
Discuss together what suffering is. Can you come up with a definition of suffering? Bear in mind that what Christians in China would consider as suffering is different to our experience, and suffering as a church body is different to individual suffering.

Read: Hebrews 12:1-13
Key verses: Hebrews 12:4-13

If we want to press on to Christian maturity, we need to *look out*. You need to look out and see the situations and difficulties God is bringing into your life to conform you into the image of Jesus. Verse 4-13 speaks of these hardships as God's discipline. God loves you and me enough to discipline us. The basic function of a parent is disciplining their children, teaching them their boundaries, teaching them that there are things that are right and wrong, good and bad. Discipline isn't just reactive: when your child's done something wrong, Pow!, here comes the discipline, but discipline is proactive too. We discipline our children in advance, we teach them things the hard way, we all learn best the hard way.

- *How many times do the words 'father' and 'son' appear in Hebrews 12:4-13? What is the author's point here?*
- *Brainstorm some of the ways God uses to discipline us.*

My son is longing to buy something in particular at the moment and he's doing a paper round to earn his money. It's going to cost him four hundred dollars and he's saved about two hundred dollars so far. He said to me the other day 'Dad, can't you lend me two hundred dollars?' I said, 'No, Matthew.' He didn't give up, 'I'll pay it you back, I will, I've worked out,' (he's twelve) 'I'll earn two hundred dollars over the next two months and I'll pay you back.' I said, 'No, Matthew, you can buy it in two months.' He said 'But the school holidays will be over in two months.' 'That's fine, you can enjoy it after the holidays.' He said, 'Why are you so hard?' I explained, 'Matthew, I want you to learn that you only buy what you can afford. If I keep paying for your things you might pay me back,' (although we've done it before and he gets slow in paying back). 'If I buy things and you pay me back, you'll grow up with the idea, "I can have anything I want and pay for it later." Debt is always expensive and you'll wish you'd learnt to buy only what you could afford. So I'm teaching you that.' So he went to his mother. She said 'What did Dad say?' 'Oh, Dad was a bit grumpy.' 'What do you mean, a bit grumpy?' 'He said "No".' 'If that's what he said, that's what I say.'

We teach our children to live within their means and as parents we teach them lots of other things as well. And the Father teaches us and one of the ways he teaches us, it says in verse 7, is 'Endure hardship as discipline'. God teaches us through hardship. Hardship is not something to be embarrassed about. We often feel, if things are tough, 'I'm embarrassed to share it with fellow Christians because maybe this is a sign of my failure or my lack of trust or my lack of faith or something.' No, it's not. Even Jesus had to learn through hardship. Hebrews 5:8 tells us: 'Although he was a son, he learned obedience from what he suffered.' This verse raises big questions; was Jesus ever disobedient? No, but his Father taught him to learn obedience. His heavenly Father taught him to learn obedience through the things he suffered. This is nothing to do with the cross; this is to do with the thirty silent years leading up to the cross. We don't know what he went through during that time but he learned obedience. None of us look for suffering and we must sympathise with those who suffer, but again and again it's God's agent in our lives for good.

● *Can all hardships be counted as discipline?*

Did you know there are some forbidden promises in the Bible? When I say forbidden, I mean we don't like to quote them; we don't put them on calendars or anything like that because we don't want to be reminded of them. Here are some of these promises: Philippians 1:29 'It has been granted to you on behalf of Christ not only to believe on him, but also to suffer for him.' Paul was writing this from prison where he was suffering and he's saying, 'It's been granted to you. God has given you not just the ability to believe on him but also to suffer for him, this is part of the package.' 1 Peter 4:19: 'So then, those who suffer according to God's will should commit themselves to their faithful Creator and continue to do good.' Not 'Those who suffer in spite of God's will because it's a fallen environment and so we've got to live with that.' We suffer according to God's will because again and again God's tool in our lives is suffering. Now let's not look at other people and say, 'Oh, God must be teaching them something.' This applies to me, it applies to you. Sympathise with those who are suffering, encourage those who suffer, relieve the suffering of others but take care that you are allowing God to mould your own heart.

● *How do these 'forbidden' verses help you in your suffering?*

There's a great verse in Romans 5, where Paul says, 'we (also) rejoice in our sufferings,' which, by the way, is not normal, is it? You can find books in almost any bookshop on how to handle your sufferings, how to overcome your problems, how to cope with your problems, how to deal with your problems but never how to rejoice in your problems. But he says, 'we also rejoice in our sufferings.' Why? 'Because we know that suffering produces perseverance; perseverance, character; and character, hope.' In my Bible I've underlined heavily those two words 'suffering produces' to remind me that suffering is productive.

● *What attitude do we need to have so that suffering produces good in our lives rather than bitterness?*

Paul, later in Romans 8, says, 'If we are children, then we are heirs – heirs of God and co-heirs with Christ, if indeed we share in his sufferings in order that we may also share in his glory.' Suffering has huge dignity in Scripture and we need to give it dignity. Paul also says, 'I consider that our present sufferings are not worth comparing with the glory that will be revealed us.' I think if you follow that through, you'll find it to be true. It's not prosperity that is the New Testament evidence of God's blessing; it is actually that we live in tough situations. And experiencing what we don't like is actually good for character growth. That's why, as Lamentations says, 'It is good for a man to bear the yoke while he is young.'

● *What do the following verses teach about the connection between suffering and glory, for Jesus and for us?*
   – *Mark 8:31*
   – *John 12:23-25*
   – *Philippians 3:10-11*
   – *1 Peter 4:13, 5:10*

When I was about sixteen I was working with somebody and I was doing a job I didn't like at all. It became obvious that I didn't like it, apparently, because the guy I was working with said to me, 'You don't like what you're doing, do you?' and I said, 'I don't, at all.' He said 'Good.' I said 'Why?' and he replied 'It will develop character in you.' I'm so glad he said that to me because I've remembered it ever since. Things you don't like often produce character. Don't duck difficulties and suffering. Romans 5:3 tells us suffering 'produces perseverance' or, as the Authorised Version says, 'tribulation works patience'.

I remember reading in one of Watchman Nee's books that one day a lady came to him and said, 'Would you pray for me?' He said, 'Certainly, what do you want to be prayed for?' She said, 'I need patience, would you pray that God would give me patience.' He said, 'Certainly.' They knelt down together. He didn't know this woman at all, and he said, 'Lord, I don't know much about this woman but I know that she has a need for patience and so I want to pray that you would bring into her life such tribulations, such difficulties, such hardships, such suffering that she won't know what to do.' While he was praying this lady got up, grabbed him by the shoulders, shook him and said, 'Stop, I've got enough of that already.' He said 'Madam, you don't understand, tribulation works patience, Romans 5:3. You want patience, you'll find it through tribulation.'

● *What does Hebrews 12:11 say discipline produces? What do these terms mean?*

Again and again hardship is God's means to bring growth and maturity into our lives. So if you want to grow, look out. I don't mean look out so that you can duck but look out at the things, the situations of life, the hardships of life that will come against you and allow them to be God's tool in moulding you and making you the person he's designed you to be.

- *What are some of the personal lessons you have learnt from suffering?*
- *Why do you think suffering is such an effective tool to make us more like Christ?*

FURTHER STUDY
Explain Colossians 1:24. Does this verse suggest that suffering has a value beyond making us more holy? Are there other Bible verses which indicate that our suffering has a wider role?

REFLECTION AND RESPONSE
Read the account of the crucifixion or watch the scene on video. As you consider your own suffering know that Jesus suffered too:

- If your body is in pain, think of Jesus' agony on the cross
- If you are suffering betrayal, think of how Judas betrayed him
- If you are depressed, remember Jesus knew such darkness, he bore the weight of our sin and was cut off from his father

Don't dwell on your hardships but spend time praying for others who are suffering:

- Pray for persecuted Christians overseas and those who have to meet in secret.
- Pray for those who are suffering in your own church. Discuss practical ways you can help them. Perhaps you could take them out for coffee, make them a meal, or look after their children for a day.

CHAPTER 14

Looking forward in hope

Aim: Seeing how hope helps us grow in Christ

FOCUS ON THE THEME
Share with the group one thing that you have really hoped for in your life. How did having hope affect your behaviour and attitudes? What was the outcome and how did you feel?

Read: Hebrews 11:1–12:13
Key verses: Hebrews 11:39-40, 12:10

Finally, if you want to press on to spiritual maturity, then *look forward*. This theme of looking forward runs throughout the whole book of Hebrews – go back to chapter 11:10 and Abraham is 'looking forward to the city with foundations, whose architect and builder is God.' Chapter 11:16 says this catalogue of men and women were 'longing for a better country'. Moses, too, was looking ahead to his reward, that's why he chose the disgrace of the people of God. The goal that kept them all looking forward and pressing on is explained in verse 12:10, 'Our fathers disciplined us for a little while as they thought best; but God disciplines us for our good, that we may share in his holiness.' With this goal in mind they persevered, (11:39), 'These were all commended for their faith, yet none of them received what had been promised.' Underlying all of this there is this ingredient in Christian living that we don't talk much about because it feels a bit of a cop-out. It's called hope.

Paul said, 'These three remain; faith, hope, and love, the greatest is love.' We agree that faith and love are pretty important but we don't talk much about hope. It sounds to us as though it implies escapism, wishful thinking; hope is a vague word to us. Actually hope has two meanings, a subjective and an objective meaning. The subjective meaning is, 'I hope it won't rain at Keswick, this week.' That's wishful thinking. If I say to you 'I hope to be back in Toronto tomorrow night,' that's not wishful thinking. I have a ticket, I have a reservation, I have a seat reserved on a plane. That's a confident expectation, I'll be home tomorrow night.

Biblical hope is not a 'I hope it won't rain at Keswick' type of hope, or a 'I hope this all turns out to be true' type of hope. Rather it's a confidence, orientating ourselves to a future confidence. I'm planning to be somewhere, sometime, I'm planning to be holy; I'm planning to be Christ-like, one day it'll all come together. In the meantime I'm in a process whereby I'm being trained, prepared and equipped for that.

- *Brainstorm together what we can be hopeful for in this life and the life to come.*

- *Look up the following verses. What more can we learn about what we are putting our hope in?*
  - *Psalm 33:18, 119:74*
  - *Lamentations 3:21-27*
  - *Romans 8:23-24*
  - *1 Corinthians 15:19*
  - *Colossians 1:27*
  - *Titus 1:2*
  - *Hebrews 6:17-20*

- *In our post-modern age where people are familiar with the subjective idea of hope, how can we explain to them the objective, biblical meaning? What examples, descriptions or images could we use?*

- *Think through the different circumstances and difficulties in your life. What difference does it make to think that they are God's training and preparation for holiness?*
- *Hope is a confident expectation that one day we will be like Christ. Our task is to orientate ourselves towards that day. What spiritual growth are you expecting and planning for in the next year:*
  - *In your own spiritual life*
  - *In the spiritual life of those in your group*
  - *With your prayer or accountability partner*

I've grown to appreciate the writings of Viktor Frankl over the last couple of years. Viktor Frankl died the day after Diana, the Princess of Wales, was killed in a road accident in Paris. I was reading through the newspaper a couple of days later and it was all full of Diana. I found one non-Diana piece of news: it was the obituary of Viktor Frankl. I'd never heard of him before. On the strength of that obituary, I went and bought one of his books and I've bought most of his books since then.

Viktor Frankl was an Austrian Jew who, in the 1930s, trained as a medical doctor in Vienna specialising in psychiatry, a field which was then in its infancy. His first job in a medical practice was to try and help attempted-suicide patients. As he sat and talked with these patients, he'd ask them, 'What caused you to want to commit suicide?' And they told him things about their past that had been the reason they had wanted to commit suicide. Frankl thought to himself, 'You know, I know people with a lot worse pasts than this who are not suicidal.' And he came to the conclusion that their problem was not actually their past at all, their problem was their future, their problem was their lack of a sense of future. And he began to develop what has become known as Logotherapy. Logo/logos is the Greek term translated in our Bibles as 'word' but which can also be translated 'meaning'. Frankl developed 'meaning therapy'. He began to develop the idea that you orientate your life around the future; some future hope, some future expectation, some future confidence. One of the questions he asked the patients who came to see him in his practice, after they'd told their story, was 'Why don't you commit suicide?' Admittedly this was not a very encouraging question for your doctor to ask but the answer gave the clue to that person's life, to that person's meaning. They'd say 'Because I've got children', 'Because I've got grandchildren,' 'Because I've got something I want to accomplish', 'Because I've got a gift I want to use.' Subsequently he wrote a book called *Man's search for meaning*[1] and I wish he could have taken it to Christ because it was so set up for Christ to step into what he wrote.

● *How has becoming a Christian given your life meaning? How is your meaning different from that of the non-Christians around you?*

In that book, *Man's search for meaning*, he tells his own story. In the 1930s he began to write on this theme and he was offered a scholarship in the United States. But he decided to stay in Austria and in the late thirties the Third Reich was growing in power and had annexed Austria. If he had gone to the United States he could have escaped persecution. But he stayed and was taken by the Nazis and put in a concentration camp; first in Dachau and then in Auschwitz. His wife, whom he'd married just before they were arrested, was killed in the gas ovens in Auschwitz and so were his parents.

In *Man's search for meaning*, he talks about the years he experienced in that concentration camp. He said 'There were those who had a vigour and a strength that others didn't have' and it was always because they were looking ahead to the future, when they would be free from the camp. 'So we'd sit around in a circle and we'd talk about what we're going to do after the war. We'd discuss the meals we would eat, we'd say "We'll come to each other's home, we'll have a meal."' They'd discuss the menu. Meanwhile they were living on watery soup that had one piece of cabbage in it. They'd say 'It's going to be wonderful. When we get out, we're going to eat like kings.' Frankl noted that these men had a new strength.

He said one day a man came to him who'd been a well-known musician. He said, 'Doctor, I had a dream and in my dream somebody appeared to me and said, "Ask me for whatever you want and I'll give it to you." And I said, "I want to know the date in which I will be free; not the date the war will be over, the date I will be free."' And Frankl said, 'And what did the man say to you?' He said, '"You'll be free on the 30th of March 1945."' It was February 1945. Frankl said, 'That man was a changed man, he had a new spring in his step, a new energy, a new vitality about him. But as we went through the month of March, March 15th, March 20th, March 24th it became obvious nobody was going to be released on March the 30th. And this man physically began to deteriorate, on the 27th March he became ill, on the 29th March he went into a coma, on the 30th March he died.' Frankl said 'They wrote on his death certificate "He died of typhus."' Frankl said 'He didn't die of typhus, he died of no hope.'

● *In what ways have non-Christians noticed your hope being expressed? When have they noticed your positive attitude, during a difficult time for example?*

The glorious thing is that no matter what situation you're in, through faith you can look beyond the circumstance and say, 'There is a city whose foundation and builder is God. That's where he's taking me, that's what he's preparing me for, that's how he's moulding me.' As you go on to maturity, as we press on, look back at the men and women who have gone before and realise their God is your God. Look up to Jesus, the author, the finisher of your faith, get to know him better, realise he, for the joy set before him, went through much more than you and I will ever go through. If you look up to Jesus, look out to your circumstances of life, the hardships, the sufferings, the persecutions that may come, the toughness of living and say, 'This is God's tool, God's hand lives behind this to mould me. He has far greater interests than my comfort, his interest is my holiness.' Then look on, look forward with hope, believing you are on a journey which it's impossible to fall away from, knowing you've been sealed forever by the Holy Spirit.

● *Looking back over Hebrews 12, what in particular has encouraged you to press on towards maturity?*

FURTHER STUDY
Look up in a concordance the occasions when Paul refers to the triad of 'faith, hope and love'. From the context, what do we learn about these Christian qualities?

REFLECTION AND RESPONSE
Confess to God the things that make you feel hopeless:
- Unemployment
- Difficult home life
- Divorce
- Financial concerns
- Church splits

Then read sections of Revelation 21 and 22 to each other. John is giving us a picture of what the future will be like; this is the certainty we base our hope on. Praise God that nothing will rob us of this glorious future. In fact Christ, the great high priest of Hebrews, is preparing us for this great day – he has made us into a royal priesthood (1 Pet. 2:5,9). Consider how you can be preparing for heaven. Think through your relationships, concerns and present priorities – how does hope give you a new perspective?

REVIEW OF THE BOOK OF HEBREWS

Consider how God the Holy Spirit wants to apply these truths to your heart, life and circumstances. What personal response is he waiting for? You may find the following prayer helpful:

'God, please do in me what you want to do in me, do all that this book talks about. Make Christ the permanent one in my life; make him the one on whom I depend to get into that land of rest. Help me to enjoy the new covenant as you put the law into my heart and my mind and you make what were commands promises for me. May I have the faith to see beyond my circumstances and see beyond conflicts. And help me to keep my eyes open; I'll look back, look up, look out and look on with the confidence that you are working in me to make me like Jesus.'

That's what holiness is. Will you ask God to be doing that? Will you ask God to make this real to you and not just the memory of a book you once read?

POINTS TO PONDER

- What have you learnt about God?
- What have you learnt about yourself?
- What actions or attitudes do you need to change as a result?

---

[1] Viktor E. Frankl, *Man's search for meaning* (Simon & Schuster, 1984)

CPSIA information can be obtained at www.ICGtesting.com
Printed in the USA
BVOW06s0617080715

407630BV00004B/11/P